SUNSHINE
FRENCH
PHRASE BOOK

By

J. ROSENBERG

PAPERFRONTS

Elliot Right Way Books
Kingswood, Surrey, U.K.

Made and Printed in Great Britain by
Hunt Barnard Printing Ltd., Aylesbury, Bucks.

CONTENTS

PART I

PART II

CONTENTS

PREFACE

THIS BOOK is intended to give a practical knowledge of conversational French, and the phrases chosen should enable visitors to French-speaking countries to express their everyday requirements.

Special attention has been paid to analysing the needs of both tourist, holidaymaker and businessman. A feature of this book is the success that has been achieved in including every phrase likely to be needed by the traveller, while still featuring handy pocket size and great ease of reference.

At the very end of the book, there is a quick-reference section showing how to get help in the event of an emergency.

HOW TO USE THIS BOOK

THE CORRECT use of a foreign language comes from habit rather than knowledge. A person could know all the rules of French Grammar, yet still be unable to speak French.

The right way to learn to speak a foreign language is to memorise the most useful words and phrases which occur over and over again. These have been arranged in part I of this book by an experienced language teacher. You have got to know these, so **learn them by heart through constant repetition.**

The second part of the book gives classified lists of useful vocabulary. Words closely related in sense have been grouped together under convenient headings to enable easy reference. The grouping of words in a logical rather than an alphabetical order has been found more suitable for beginners.

There is no need to learn all the words in the second part by heart. They can be looked up when needed and combined with the phrases given in Part I. Thus the student who was memorising the French for 'I would like to', 'Would you like to?', 'Where can I find . . .?', 'Please show me . . .', etc., has a stock of correct language forms at his command which he can enlarge as occasion arises from the lists provided in the second part of the book. He can further extend his vocabulary by use of a good dictionary.

FRENCH PRONUNCIATION

LE CONGRÈS DU PARTI SOCIALISTE
Les difficultes de l'industrie du cinéma francais
LES CREDITS SUPPLEMENTAIRES POUR LA DEFENSE
NATIONALE
Deux nouvelles expeditions au pole Nord
UNE PRINCESSE EPOUSE UN CHAUFFEUR

Here are five headlines taken from French Newspapers. Even with no knowledge of French at all, it is not difficult to recognise these sentences as meaning:

The Congress of the Socialist Party
The Difficulties of the French Cinema Industry
Supplementary Credits for National Defence
Two New Expeditions to the North Pole
A Princess marries a Chauffeur

Many French words are similar to English ones, and it is sometimes possible, with a little guesswork, to make out the sense of many words and sentences in French books or newspapers.

But if you read them to a Frenchman, or he to you, there would be complete bewilderment, because neither of you would understand what the other was saying. Although the spelling of words is sometimes alike or similar, their pronunciation is completely different in the two languages. Let us examine these headlines one by one:

Le Congrès du Parti Socialiste

le (=the) is pronounced like the italicized part of the word mil*ler*, that is to say, the 'e' is just a faint sound, such as you get in the words 'hatter,' 'baker,' 'bitter', and it should be uttered as rapidly as possble.

congrès. The first syllable is very much like 'cong' in the English word 'congress,' but the French make it a nasal sound, i.e. as much air as possible must escape through the nosé and the 'ng' must not be sounded at all. In our system of imitated pronunciation the nasal sound is indicated by a capital 'N.' It is not really a consonant, but merely an indication that the preceding vowel is a nasal.

The second syllable of the word 'congrès' is pronounced like the italicized part of the English word '*grain*.' French 'è' is always pronounced like English 'ai' (as in 'pair'), and the final 's,' like most final consonants, is not sounded at all. In our imitated pronunciation we therefore show the word 'congrès' as *koN-grai*.

du (= of the) has a vowel sound which has no English counterpart.

It is not difficult to acquire. If you say 'dee' with your lips protruded as if you were going to whistle, you will get the right sound. As the French 'u' is nothing but 'ee' said with rounded lips, we describe this sound in our imitated pronunciation as (*ee*), indicating by the brackets that the lips have to be rounded while saying 'ee'.

parti (= party) is sounded like *pahr-tee*, with equal stress on both syllables.

socialiste is pronounced *so-see-ah-leest*, with equal stress on each of the four syllables.

LES DIFFICULTES DE L'INDUSTRIE DU CINÉMA FRANÇAIS

les (= the, plural) is pronounced as *lay*.

difficultés as if it were spelt *dee fe-k(ee)l-tay*, with equal stress on each syllable. Remember that (*ee*) is 'ee' with rounded lips.

de (=of), like the italicized part of 'har*der*.'

l'industrie. The first syllable of this word contains another nasal sound. It is very similar to the italicized part of the word '*lan*guage,' but again with more breath escaping through the nose and without sounding the 'ng' at all. This nasal sound is the nasal counterpart to the 'ai' sound described above. It is rendered in our imitated pronunciation as *aiN*. The 'du' part of 'industrie' is as described above, and French 'ie' is sounded as in English 'field,' so that the whole word can be transcribed as *laiN-d(ee)s-tree*.

du as shown previously.

cinéma is pronounced like *see-nay-mah*, with equal stress on each of the three syllables.

français [*fraN-sai*] brings us to another nasal sound. Its nearest English counterpart would be the vowel heard in the English word 'frump,' but again with as much air as you can let escape through the nose. It is the same sound as heard at the end of the French word 'restaurant,' which is pronounced *rais-toh-raN*.

LES CRÉDITS SUPPLÉMENTAIRES POUR LA DÉFENSE NATIONALE

les (plural 'the') is pronounced as *lay*.

crédits sounds like *cray-dee*.

supplémentaires is pronounced *s(ee)p-lay-maN-tair*, i.e. *seep* with lips protruded, *maN* with the nasal 'a' as in 'français,' 'restaurant,' etc.; *tair* is sounded very much like the English word 'tare.'

pour (=fɔr) is pronounced *poor* (but not *poo-er*), the 'r' following a pure 'oo' sound.

la as in English '*last.*'

défense should be pronounced as *day-faNs*.

nationale is pronounced *nahs-you-hanl* (say *nas* as in '*na*sty,' *yon* as in '*yon*der,' *al* as in 'chor*ale*').

DEUX NOUVELLES EXPEDITIONS AU PÔLE NORD

deux (=two). This word contains another vowel sound for which there exists no English counterpart. If you say 'day' with your lips rounded, the resulting sound will be the correct pronunciation of the French word 'deux.' The final 'x' is not sounded. Similarly, if you say 'blay' with rounded lips, you get the French word 'bleu,' which means 'blue.' In our imitated pronunciation we indicate this sound by (*ay*).

nouvelles (=new) is pronounced *noo-vel*, the *el* as in '*el*m.'

expéditions sounds like *aiks-pay-dees-yoN*, with equal stress on all four syllables.

au (=to the) is pronounced like 'oh!'

Pôle Nord (=North Pole), say *pol* as in '*pol*ice,' followed by *nor* as in '*Nor*wich.'

UNE PRINCESSE ÉPOUSE UN CHAUFFEUR

une (=a, feminine) is pronounced (*ee*)*n*, the 'ee' with rounded lips as explained above.

princesse. The first syllable of 'princesse' sounds like the English word 'prank,' not sounding the 'k.' The second syllable is pronounced the same as in the English word 'princess.'

épouse (=marries) is pronounced *ay-pooz* and rhymes with 'whose.'

un chauffeur [(ai)N *shoh-f(ai)r*] (=a chauffeur). The first part of the word 'chauffeur' is pronounced as in English, i.e. like the word 'show.' The second syllable is very similar to the English word 'fir.' The difference between the English and the French pronunciation is that in English you stress the first syllable and mumble the second. In the French pronunciation of the word both syllables get equal stress: 'show-fir.'

The 'un' brings us to the last of the four nasal sounds. It is the nasal counterpart to the 'ir' sound just described. Try to pass as much air as you can through your nose while making the vowel sound of English her, sir or fur.

In our imitated pronunciation we describe the 'ir' sound by (ai) because it is the 'ai' sound (as in 'pair') pronounced with rounded lips. If you say 'pair' with rounded lips you get the correct pronunciation of the French word 'peur' which means 'fear.' Its nasal counterpart, which you encounter in such words as parfum, Verdun, lundi (=Monday), etc., is shown as (ai)N.

The sentences given here should be studied very carefully, as they contain all the French sounds that have no counterparts in English. They are (*ee*), (*ay*) and (*ai*), which are *ee*, *ay* and *ai* pronounced with rounded lips, as well as the four nasals which in our system of imitated pronunciation are rendered by *aN*, *aiN*, *oN* and (*ai*)*N*.

To speak French correctly, it is not enough to know how to pronounce the French sounds. Stress and intonation are also entirely different from English. The most important differences are:

1. All the syllables of French words are evenly pronounced with a slight stress on the last syllable. For instance, in the word **britannique**, which is pronounced *bree-tah-neek*, the pitch of the voice is raised at the end.

2. French is spoken with more emphasis than English, the lips and the tongue are more mobile, and there must be no mumbling or slurring together of syllables. Take, for instance, the word 'national,' which is common to both languages. It is a word of three syllables, but in colloquial English it is reduced to one: 'nashnl.' In the French word all three syllables are fully pronounced: *nahs-yoh-nahl*.

RÉSUMÉ OF THE IMITATED PRONUNCIATION SYSTEM USED IN THIS BOOK

    ah   like the 'a' in 'father'
    ai   as in 'pair'

(ai)	the same with rounded lips
ay	as in 'tray'
(ay)	the same with rounded lips
ee	as in 'see'
(ee)	the same with rounded lips
e	as in 'open'
o	as in 'not'
oh	as in 'note'
aN	nasal 'ah'
oN	nasal 'o'
aiN or *iN*	nasal 'ai'
(ai)N or *uN*	nasal '(ai)'
g	as in 'go'
s	as in 'so'
y	as in 'yes'
zh	like the 's' in 'measure'

Those not given above to be pronounced as in English.

Sometimes we English simply do not realise how difficult our language is for a foreigner to read. Ponder for a moment upon the words **bough, rough, cough** and **through**. The same spelling, but no less than four completely different pronunciations.

French is a much more precise language, and with **very** few exceptions, pronunciation is according to the following rules:

a, à	as in 'far,' but cut short
â	as in 'father,' mouth wide open
au	like the *o* of 'go'
c	before *a*, *o*, *i* and before consonants, as in 'cat'
	before *e*, *i* and *y*, like the *s* in 'so'
ç	like the *s* of 'so'
ch	like the *sh* of 'ship'
e	at the end of a word or syllable, as a faint murmur sound, like the *a* in 'ago' or the *e* of 'open';
	if followed by a mute consonant at the end of a word, like the *a* in 'hate';
	if followed by a sounded consonant, as in 'let'
é	like the *a* in 'hate'

è, ê, ei, ai, ay   like the *ai* in 'pair'

eau   same as *au*

eu   like no English sound. Say *ay* with rounded lips (*ay*). When at the end of a word followed by a consonant which is not silent, like the *ir* in 'sir,' but with rounded lips; e.g. 'deux' is pronounced *d(ay)*, because the final *x* is silent, but 'neuf' is pronounced *n(ai)f*, as the *f* is sounded (compare the paragraph below on Silent Letters).

g   before *a, o, u* and before consonants, as in 'go'; before *e* and *i*, like the *s* in 'pleasure.'

gn   like *ni* in 'onion'

gu   like the *g* in 'go'

ge   like the *s* in 'pleasure'

h   is not pronounced at all

i, î   like *ee* in 'see,' but very short and tense

j   like the *s* in 'pleasure'

l   as in 'lamp'

o   as in 'not'

ô   as in 'note'

œ   same as *eu*

oi   like *wa* in 'wagon'

ou, où, oû   like *oo* in 'root'
     qu   like *k*
      r   pronounced as by Scottish people, even at the end of a
             word
      s   usually as in 'so';
             between vowels, as in 'rose'
      u   has no English counterpart. Say *ee* with your lips rounded

Sounds not shown above are generally as in English

NASALS

Whenever a vowel comes before *m* or *n* it becomes a nasal. There are four nasals:

an (sometimes *am*, *en* or *em*);

on or *om*;

in (sometimes *im*, *ain*, *aim*, *en*, *ein* or *eim*);

un or *um*.

How these sounds are produced has been explained on page 15.

Note.—There is no nasal sound if *n* or *m* are followed by a vowel or doubled, e.g. 'une' is pronounced (*ee*)n, 'somme' = *som*, etc.

SILENT LETTERS

Consonants at the end of a word are generally silent with the exception of *c*, *f*, *l* and *r*. They are sounded, however, if followed by a word beginning with a vowel, but only if the following word is closely connected in sense with the preceding and there is no pause between the two words (compare English 'ham and eggs,' which sounds like one word: 'hamaneggs'); e.g. in 'deux portes' the *x* is silent, because the following letter is a consonant, but 'deux amis' is pronounced *d(ay)-zah-mee*, because 'deux' is followed by a vowel, the *x* is sounded and the two words are joined together.

FRENCH GRAMMAR

For those really interested in the study of French Grammar, there are many excellent books on the subject available. What has been done here is to analyse the amount of grammatical knowledge that is really necessary for the beginner or occasional traveller. It really turns out to be very little, and the basics are given in the next few pages.

Masculine and Feminine

In French, the names of things as well as the names of persons are either
masculine or feminine, and they are referred to as either 'he' or 'she.'

	Masculine			*Feminine*	
le père	*le pair*	the father	la mère	*lah mair*	the mother
le frère	*le frair*	the brother	la sœur	*lah s(ai)r*	the sister
le livre	*le leevr*	the book	la table	*lah tahbl*	the table
le col	*le kol*	the collar	la manche	*lah maNsh*	the sleeve

The word for 'the' in French is *le* before a masculine noun and *la* before
a feminine. There are some practical rules for knowing which nouns are
masculine and which are feminine. They will be found on page 122.
As these rules do not cover all nouns, the best way is always to learn the
noun together with the Definite Article (*le* or *la*).

He and She

le père; il est grand	*le pair; ee-lai graN*	the father; he is tall
la mère; elle est grande	*la mair ai-lai graNd*	the mother; she is tall
le fils; il est petit	*le fees; ee-lai p'tee*	the son; he is small
la fille; elle est petite	*lah feey; ai-lai p'teet*	the daughter; she is small

Note from the above examples that adjectives have masculine and feminine forms. To obtain the feminine form of an adjective 'e' is added to the masculine. This 'e' is mute, but it causes a final consonant to be sounded. Compare the following:

Masculine		Feminine		
vert	*vair*	verte	*vairt*	green
brun	*br(ai)N*	brune	*br(ee)n*	brown
rouge	*roozh*	rouge	*roozh*	red
joli	*zho-lee*	jolie	*zho-lee*	pretty
beau	*boh*	belle	*bail*	beautiful
bon	*boN*	bonne	*bon*	good
blanc	*blaN*	blanche	*blaNsh*	white

Note.—1. Adjectives ending in 'e' have the same form, whether they are masculine or feminine.

2. Adjectives ending in a vowel (other than mute 'e') add 'e' for the feminine. This, however, does not affect their pronunciation.

3. Some adjectives have more or less irregular feminine forms.

Singular and Plural

le mur *le m(ee)r* the wall	**les murs** *lay m(ee)r* the walls
la porte *lah port* the door	**les portes** *lay port* the doors
l'enfant *laN-faN* the child	**les enfants** *lay-zaN-faN* the children
le Français *le fraN-sai* the Frenchman	**les Français** *lay fraN-sai* the Frenchmen; the French
la Française *lah fraN-saiz* the Frenchwoman	**les Françaises** *lay fraN-saiz* the Frenchwomen
l'Anglais *laN-glai* the Englishman	**les Anglais** *lay-zaN-glai* the Englishmen; the English
l'Anglaise *laN-glaiz* the Englishwoman	**les Anglaises** *lay-zaN-glaiz* the Englishwomen
le petit garçon *le p'tee gahr-soN* the little boy	**les petits garçons** *lay p'tee gahr-soN* the little boys
la petite fille *lah p'teet feey* the little girl	**les petites filles** *lay p'teet feey* the little girls

Note.—1. Nouns and adjectives in the plural take the ending 's'. This 's' is mute.

2. Before any plural noun, whether masculine or feminine, the word for 'the' in French is *les*.

3. *le* and *la* are replaced by *l'* before vowel.

It and They

le crayon; il est bleu	*le krai-yoN; ee-lai bl(ay)*	the pencil; it is blue
la plume; elle est jaune	*lah pl(ee)m; ai-lai zhohn*	the pen; it is yellow
les mouchoirs; ils sont blancs	*lay lay moosh-wahr; eel soN blaN*	the handkerchiefs; they are white
les nappes; elles sont blanches	*lay nahp; ail soN blaNsh*	the tablecloths; they are white

Masculine		*Feminine*		
Sing.	*Plur.*	*Sing.*	*Plur.*	
le	les	la	les	the
il	ils	elle	elles	it, they

Special care must be taken with the translation of 'it' and 'they.'
Use: *il* when 'it' stands for a masculine noun in singular.
     elle when 'it' stands for a feminine noun in singular.
     ils when 'they' stands for masculine nouns in plural.
     elles when 'they' stands for feminine nouns in plural.

For example, when translating ('it is green' 'it' referring to the book, which is *le livre*, i.e. masculine in French), the word *il* is used for the translation of 'it': *il est vert*. But when 'it' stands for the door, which is *la porte,* i.e. feminine, *elle* is used for the translation of 'it', as in: *elle est verte.*

A, An
Masculine

un jardin	*(ai)N zhahr-daiN*	a garden
un journal	*(ai)N zhoor-nahl*	a newspaper
un cigare	*(ai)N see-gahr*	a cigar

Feminine

une maison	*(ee)n mai-zoN*	a house
une chaise	*(ee)n shaiz*	a chair
une cigarette	*(ee)n see-gah-rait*	a cigarette

Plural

des Français	*day fraN-sai*	Frenchmen; French people
des allumettes	*day-zah-l(ee)mait*	matches
des journaux	*day zhoor-noh*	newspapers

Note.—1. *Un,* 'a', 'an,' is used before a masculine noun.

2. *Une,* 'a,' 'an,' is used before a feminine noun.

3. In plural, where there is no article at all in English (books, horses,

Englishmen), the French use a special form, *des*, which also means 'some' or 'any.'

4. Words ending in 'al' have their plural in 'aux' (pronounced *oh*).

To be and Not to be

être *aitr* to be	ne pas être *ne pah-zaitr* not to be	
je suis content	*zhe swee koN-taN*	I am glad
vous êtes fatigué	*voo-zait fah-tee-gay*	You are tired
il est malade	*ee-lai mah-lahd*	He is ill
elle est belle	*ai-lai bail*	She is beautiful
nous sommes prêts	*noo som prai*	We are ready
ils sont Anglais	*eel soN-taN-glai*	They (masc.) are English
elles sont Anglaises	*ail soN-taN-glaiz*	They (fem.) are English
suis-je en retard?	*swee zhe aN re-tahr*	Am I late?
êtes-vous là?	*ait voo lah*	Are you there?
est-il Écossais?	*ai-teel ay-kò-sai*	Is he a Scot?
est-elle Française	*ai-tail fraN-saiz*	Is she French?
sommes-nous tous ici?	*som noo toos ee-see*	Are we all here?
sont-ils Belges?	*soN-teel bailzh*	Are they (masc.) Belgians?
sont-elles Suisses?	*soN-tail swees*	Are they (fem.) Swiss?

Order of Words

A foreign language is not a word-for-word rendering of your own. Most things are expressed differently and the order of words in a sentence is not always the same. Sometimes more words are required to express the same idea, sometimes fewer.

Do you speak? is **Parlez-vous?** (=Speak you?) (*pahr-lɔy voo*).

I am not speaking **Je ne parle pas** (*zhe ne pahrl pah*).

He is sleeping is **Il dort** (*eel dor*).

Note from the above examples that:

1. The verb 'to do' is not used in French to form questions or to make negative statements.

2. No difference is made between 'she does not speak' and 'she is not speaking': *elle ne parle pas* translates both.

Rules of gender

THE only safe rule is to learn the gender with the noun, not 'plume,' but 'la plume,' not 'arbre,' but 'un arbre,' not 'hôtel,' but 'un hôtel'; i.e. to learn each noun with the definite article (or the indefinite when the noun begins with a vowel or *h* mute). It is best to learn the noun accompanied not only by the article but also by an adjective; e.g. 'la grande maison'; 'le petit jardin'; 'un bon dîner,'' etc.

This—the only safe method of learning genders—may be usefully supplemented by the following rules, which, however, do not cover all nouns.

MASCULINE

1. *Nouns denoting male beings*
   Examples: le professeur, the teacher   le lion, the lion
             le garçon, the waiter   le chien, the dog

   Exceptions: une personne, a person   une sentinelle, a sentry
              une recrue, a recruit   une victime, a victim

2. *Names of seasons, months and days*
   Examples:
   au printemps, in spring   un été chaud, a hot summer
   janvier dernier, last January   le mardi suivant, the following Tuesday

3. *Names of trees and shrubs*
   Examples:
      un arbre fruitier, a fruit tree   le hêtre, the beech
      un arbuste, shrub   le chèvrefeuille, honeysuckle

   Exceptions: la vigne, vine   la bruyère, heather
               la ronce, bramble

4. *Words ending in 'age,' 'al,' 'eau,' 'er,' 'i,' 'ier,' 'ment,' 'oir'*

    Examples: le langage, language   le journal, newspaper
             le château, castle   le verger, orchard
             le cri, shout   un officier, officer
             le gouvernement, government   le couloir, corridor
    Exceptions: la fourmi, ant   la jument, mare

Note.—In the following words 'age' and 'eau' are not terminations:

    la cage, cage   une image, picture   la page, page
    la plage, beach   la nage, swimming
    la peau, skin   l'eau (f.), water

5. *Most nouns ending in a consonant*

    Examples: le lac, lake   le bois, wood   le sel, salt
    Exceptions: la clef, key   la croix, cross   la dent, tooth
                la faim, hunger   la fin, end   la fleur, flower
                la forêt, forest   la main, hand   la mer, sea
                la nuit, night   la soif, thirst   la voix, voice

FEMININE

1. *Female beings*

la couturière, dressmaker　　　**la lionne,** lioness

Note.—(1) Professions not usually followed by women are masculine, even when they refer to women; e.g. 'elle est un grand poète,' she is a great poet. A woman doctor is 'une femme docteur,' a woman writer 'une femme écrivain,' etc.

(2) Most masculine nouns denoting male beings have a corresponding feminine gender formed by adding 'e' mute: le marquis, la marquise; un orphelin (orphan), une orpheline; le couturier, la couturière, etc.

Nouns ending in "e" mute remain unchanged, but take the feminine article (except in the case of professions usually followed by men): un élève (pupil), une élève; un artiste, une artiste, etc. Some take a feminine in 'esse': le nègre (negro), la négresse; le tigre, la tigresse; le maître (master), la maîtresse; and others.

Nouns ending in 'eur' change into 'euse': le danseur (dancer), la danseuse; le coiffeur (hairdresser), la coiffeuse, etc.

Nouns in 'teur' change this ending into 'trice'; un acteur (actor), une actrice; un spectateur (spectator), une spectatrice, etc.

Nouns ending in 'en,' 'on,' 't' double the final consonant besides adding 'e' mute: le citoyen (citizen), la citoyenne; le lion, la lionne; le chat (cat), la chatte.

2. *Nouns ending in 'tion'*

         la nation, nation   la révolution, revolution

3. *Most nouns ending in 'e'*

la robe, dress	la sortie, exit	une année, year

Exceptions:

le crime, crime	le doute, doubt	le fleuve, river
le livre, book	le monde, world	le nombre, number
un ange, angel	le beurre, butter	le légume, vegetable
le peigne, comb	le rêve, dream	le siège, seat·
le sucre, sugar	le verre, glass	le timbre, stamp

WORDS SPELLED ALIKE BUT OF DIFFERENT GENDER

le livre, book	la livre, pound
le manche, handle	la manche, sleeve
le page, page-boy	la page, page (of a book)
le poêle, stove	la poêle, frying pan
le poste, situation, post	la poste, post-office
le tour, trick, turn	la tour, tower
le voile, veil	la voile, sail

Part I
Essential Phrases

GREETING AND LEAVE-TAKING

THE French are extremely polite. It is considered rude to answer merely oui or non. Every oui or non is followed by either monsieur (when talking to a man), or madame (to a married woman), or mademoiselle (to an unmarried woman).

The same applies to greetings. 'Good day' (or 'Good morning,' or 'Good afternoon') is Bonjour (*boN-zhoor*), monsieur (*miss-y(ay)*), or madame (*mah-dahm*), or mademoiselle (*mahd-mwah-zail*).

'Good evening' is Bonsoir (*boN-swahr*) monsieur (madame, mademoiselle).

'Good night' is Bonne nuit (*bon nwee*) monsieur (madame, mademoiselle).

'Goodbye' or 'Cheerio' is Au revoir (*oh re-vwahr*) monsieur (madame, mademoiselle).

A demain	*ah d'maiN*	Till to-morrow
A ce soir	*ah se swahr*	Till this evening
A bientôt	*ah byaiN-toh*	Till soon (i.e. see you soon; so long)

THANKS AND APOLOGIES

Merci	*mair-see*	Thanks
Merci beaucoup	*mair-see boh-koo*	Thanks very much
Vous êtes bien aimable	*voo-zait byai-nai-mahbl*	You are very kind
Je vous remercie	*zh'voo re-mair-see*	I thank you
Il n'y a pas de quoi	*eel nyah pah de kwah*	Don't mention it (lit. 'There is not of what')

Note.—If you are offered anything and wish to accept: **avec plaisir** (*ah-vaik plai-zeer*) with pleasure; **vous êtes bien aimable** (see above). If you refuse, say: **merci** or **merci bien.**

Pardon	*pahr-doN*	Sorry
Excusez-moi	*aiks-k(ee)-zay mwah*	Excuse me

Je vous demande pardon	zh'voo d'maNd pahr-doN	I beg your pardon; I apologize
Je regrette beaucoup	zhe re-grait boh-koo	I am very sorry
Pardonnez-moi	pahr-do-nay mwah	Forgive me

Note.—For 'I beg your pardon' in the sense of "Please repeat what you said; I did not understand you very well,' say: **Plaît-il?** (*plai-teel*) or **Vous dîtes?** (*voo deet*).

APPROVAL AND DISAPPROVAL

Oui	wee	Yes
Non	noN	No
Bon	boN	Good! All right!
Très bien	trai byaiN	Very well
C'est ça	sai sah	That's it. That's right
C'est vrai	sai vrai	That's true
C'est beau	sai boh	it's beautiful
C'est joli	sai zho-lee	It's pretty
C'est merveilleux	sai mair -vai-y(ay)	It's wonderful
C'est délicieux	sai day-lees-y(ay)	It's delicious

C'est drôle	*sai drohl*	It's funny
Ce n'est pas mal	*s'nai pah mahl*	It is not bad
Ce n'est pas bon	*s'nai pah boN*	It is not good
Ce n'est pas vrai	*s'nai pah vrai*	It is not true
Je sais	*zhe sai*	I know
Je ne sais pas	*zhen'sai pah*	I don't know
Je comprends	*zhe koN-praN*	I understand
Je ne comprends pas	*zhen'koN-praN pah*	I don't understand
Je l'aime	*zhe laim*	I like it
Je ne l'aime pas	*zhe ne laim pah*	I don't like it
Certainement	*sair-tain-maN*	Certainly
Certainement pas	*sair-tain-maN pah*	Certainly not
Naturellement	*nah-t(ee)-rail'maN*	Naturally. Of course
Naturellement pas	*nah-t(ee)-rail'maN pah*	Of course not!
Peut-être	*p(ay)-taitr*	Perhaps. Maybe
Pas du tout	*pah d(ee) too*	Not at all
Si vous voulez	*see voo voo-lay*	If you like
Ça m'est égal	*sah mai-tai-gahl*	It's all the same to me Just as you like
Je le crois	*zhe le krwah*	I believe so
Je l'espère	*zhe lais-pair*	I hope so
Ça dépend	*sah day-paN*	It depends

D'accord!	dah-kor	Agreed. All right. O.K.
Il est gentil	ee-lai zhaN-tee	He is nice
Ils sont gentils	eel soN zhaN-tee	They are nice (m.)
Elle est gentille	ai-lai zhaN-teey	She is nice
Elles sont gentilles	ail soN zhaN-teey	They are nice (f.)
C'est mauvais	sai moh-vai	It is bad
sale	sahl	dirty
horrible	o-reebl	horrible
dégoutant	day-goo-taN	disgusting
laid	lai	ugly
Vous n'êtes pas du tout aimable	voo nait pah d(ee) too ai-mahbl	You are not at all kind

QUESTIONS AND ANSWERS

Venez-vous?	ve-nay voo	Are you coming?
Mangez-vous?	maN-zhay voo	Are you eating?
Dormez-vous?	dor-may voo	Are you sleeping?
Jouez-vous?	zhoo-ay voo	Are you playing?
Vous venez (n'est-ce pas?)	voo v'nay (nais pah)	You are coming, aren't you?

| Oui, je viens | *wee zhe vyiN* | Yes, I am coming |
| Non, je ne viens pas | *noN zh'ne vyiN pah* | No, I am not coming |

Ne... pas = not. Ne precedes the verb and pas follows it.

Êtes-vous Français(e)?	*ait voo fraN-sai(z)*	Are you French?
occupé(e)?	*oh-k(ee)pay*	busy?
libre?	*leebr*	free?
prêt(e)?	*prai(t)*	ready?
fatigué(e)?	*fah-tee-gay*	tired?
malade?	*mah-lahd*	ill?

| Vous êtes Française(e), n'est-ce pas? | *voo-sait fraN-sai(z) nais pah* | You are French, aren't you? |

The letters in parentheses are added when speaking of women.

| Je suis Français(e) | *zhe s(w)ee fraN-sai(z)* | I am French |
| Non, je ne viens pas | *noN zhe ne vyiN pah* | No, I am not coming |

Where? Où? *oo*

Où est-il?	*oo ai-teel*	Where is he?
Mon ami, où est-il?	*mo-nah-mee oo ai-teel*	Where is my friend?
Mes amis, où sont-ils?	*may-zah-mee oo soN-teel*	Where are my friends?
Où est-elle?	*oo ai-tail*	Where is she?
Madame Albert, où est-elle?	*mah-dahm ahl-bair oo ai-tail*	Where is Mrs. Albert?
Mademoiselle, où est-elle?	*mahd-mwah-zail oo ai-tail*	Where is the young lady?
Les jeunes filles, où sont-elles?	*lay zh(ai)n feey oo soN-tail*	Where are the girls?
Les lampes, où sont-elles?	*lay laNP oo soN-tail*	Where are the lamps?
Où êtes-vous?	*oo ait voo*	Where are you?
Où sommes-nous?	*oo som noo*	Where are we?
Où allez-vous?	*oo ah-lay voo*	Where are you going?
D'où venez-vous?	*doo v-nay voo*	Where do you come from?
Où est la gare?	*oo ai lah gahr*	Where is the station?
le bureau de poste?	*le b(ee)roh de post*	the post office?

Who? Qui? *kee*, or Qui est-ce qui? *kee ais kee*

Qui est le patron?	*kee ai le paht-roN*	Who is the master of the place (the boss)?
Qui est-ce?	*kee ais*	Who is it?
Qui est là?	*kee ai lah*	Who is there?
Qui est cet homme?	*kee ai sai-tom*	Who is that man?
Qui est cette femme?	*kee ai sait fahm*	Who is that woman?
Qui sont ces hommes?	*kee soN sai-zom*	Who are these men?
Qui sont ces femmes?	*kee soN sai fahm*	Who are these women?
Qui voyez-vous?	*kee vwah-yay voo*	Whom do you see?
Qui sait ça?	*kee sai sah*	Who knows that?
Qui dit ça?	*kee dee sah*	Who says that?
De qui parlez-vous?	*de kee pahr-lay voo*	Of whom are you speaking?
A qui parlez-vous?	*ah kee pahr-lay voo*	To whom are you speaking?
A qui est-ce?	*ah kee ais*	To whom does this belong?
Pour qui est-ce?	*poor kee ais*	For whom is it?
Avec qui vont-ils	*ah-vaik kee voN-teel*	With whom do they
(t l)?	*(t il)*	go?

What? Que? *ke*, or Qu'est-ce que? *kais-ke*

Qu'est-ce que c'est?	*kaisk'sai*	What is it?
Qu'est-ce que	*kaisk'*	What
vous dites?	*voo deet*	do you say?
vous faites?	*voo fait*	are you doing?
vous mangez?	*voo maN-zhay*	are you eating?
vous voulez?	*voo voo-lay*	do you want?
vous avez?	*voo-zah-vay*	have you?
il dit?	*eel dee*	does he say?
elle fait?	*ail fai*	is she doing?
ils mangent?	*eel maNzh*	are they eating?
elles boivent?	*ail bwahv*	are they (f.) drinking?
il y a?	*eel yah*	is the matter?

Alternative forms with *que* are: Que dites-vous? Que faites-vous? Que mangez-vous? Que buvez-vous? Qu'avez-vous? Que dit-il? etc..

Note.—'What' in the combinations 'with what,' 'of what,' 'to what,' etc., is quoi *kwah*:

Avec quoi?	*ah-vaik kwah*	With what?

Derrière quoi?	*dair-yair kwah*	Behind what?
De quoi?	*de kwah*	Of what? From what?
A quoi?	*ah kwah*	To what?

Which? What? What a . . .! Quel[1] Quelle[2] Quels[3] Quelles[4]
kail (these four forms are pronounced alike)

1 With a masculine noun (singular).   3 With masculine nouns (plural).
2 With a feminine noun (singular).   4 With feminine nouns (plural).

Quel jour sommes-nous?	*kail zhoor som noo*	What day are we? (What's to-day?)
Quelle heure est-il?	*kai-l(ai)r ai-teel*	What time is it?
A quelle heure	*ah kai-l(ai)r*	At what time
partez-vous?	*pahr-tay voo*	are you leaving?
vient-il?	*vyiN-teel*	is he coming?
viennent-ils?	*vyiN-teel*	are they coming?
Quel est votre nom?	*kai-lai votr noN*	What is your name?
Quel est le nom de	*kai-lai le noN de*	What is the name of
cette ville?	*sait veel*	this town?
ce village?	*se vee-lahzh*	this village?
cet endroit?	*sai-taN-drwah*	this place?
Quel vilain temps!	*kail vee-liN taN*	What nasty weather!

Quel beau temps!	*kail boh taN*	What a beautiful day!
Quelle belle église!	*kail bai-lay-gleez*	What a beautiful church!
Quels beaux enfants!	*kail boh-zaN-faN*	What beautiful children!
Quelles belles fleurs!	*kail bail fl(ai)r*	What beautiful flowers!

Note.—There is no difference in French between 'what a ...!' 'which ...' and 'what ...' when used as an adjective, i.e. in connection with nouns. As with all adjectives, there is a special form for the feminine, and in plural an *s* is added.

How much? How many? Combien? *koN-byaiN*

Combien de kilo-mètres?	*koN-byaiN de kee-loh-maitr*	How many kilo-metres?
Combien d'argent?	*koN-byaiN dahr-zhaN*	How much money?
Combien d'hommes	*koN-byaiN dom*	How many men?
Combien en avez vous?	*koN-byaiN-aN-nah-vay voo*	How much (or many) have you got?
Combien en voulez-vous?	*koN-byaiN-aN voo-lay voo*	How much (or many) do you want?

Combien de temps?	*koN-byaiN de taN*	How much time? (How long?)
Combien est-ce?	*koN-byaiN ai-se*	How much is it?

When? Quand? *kaN*

Quand vient-il?	*kaN vyaiN-teel*	When is he coming?
Quand viennent-ils?	*kaN vyain-teel*	When are they coming?
Quand partez-vous?	*kaN pahr-tay voo*	When are you leaving?
Quand revenez-vous?	*KaN rev' nay voo*	When are you coming back?
Quand reviennent-ils?	*kaN rev-yain-teel*	When are they coming back?

Why? Pourquoi? *poor-kwah*

Pourquoi faites-vous ça?	*poor-kwah fait voo sah*	Why do you do that?
Pourquoi dites-vous ça?	*poor-kwah deet voo sah*	Why do you say that?
Pourquoi partez-vous déjà?	*poor-kwah pahr-tay voo day-zhah*	Why are you leaving already?
Pourquoi ça?	*poor-kwah sah*	What is the reason of that?

Pourquoi pas?	*poor-kwah pah*	Why not?
	How? Comment? *ko-maN*	
Comment ça va?	*ko-maN sah vah*	How is it going? (How are you?)
Comment va	*ko-maN vah*	How is
monsieur votre père?	*miss-y(ay) votr pair*	your father?
madame votre mère?	*mah-dahm votr mair*	your mother?
Mademoiselle?	*mahd-mwah-zail*	the young lady?
votre fils?	*votr fees*	your son?
Comment vont	*ko-maN voN*	How are
les petits?	*lay p'tee*	the little ones?
vos frères?	*voh frair*	your brothers?
vos sœurs?	*voh s(ai)r*	your sisters?
Comment dites-vous?	*ko-maN deet voo*	What's that you are saying? What did you say?
Comment ça?	*ko-maN sah*	How's that? How do you mean?

Miscellaneous Questions

Est-ce que *aisk'* (is it that), when placed before a statement turns it into a question, e.g.:

Elle est Française	*ai-lai fraN saiz*	She is French.
Est-ce qu'elle est Française?	*ais kai-lai fraN-saiz*	Is she French?
[1]Est-ce que vous venez?	*aisk' voo ve-nay*	Are you coming?
[1]Est-ce que vous parlez français?	*aisk' voo-pahr-lay fraN-sai*	Do you speak French?

1 Alternative forms to these questions are: Venez-vous? Parlez-vous français?

[1]Est-ce que vous comprenez?	*aisk' voo koN-pre-nay*	Do you understand?
[1]Est-ce que vous pouvez faire ça?	*aisk' voo poo-vay fair sah*	Can you do that?
[1]Est-ce que vous pouvez réparer ça?	*aisk' voo poo-vay ray-pah-ray sah*	Can you repair that?

1 Alternative forms to these questions are: Comprenez-vous? Pouvez-vous faire ça? Pouvez-vous réparer ça? etc.

Est-ce que vous pouvez me donner ça?	*aisk' voo poo-vay me do-nay sah*	Can you give me that?
Est-ce que vous pouvez me prêter ça?	*aisk' voo poo-vay me prai-tay sah*	Can you lend me that?
Est-ce que vous avez du pain? de l'eau? des cigarettes?	*aisk' voo-zah-vay d(ee) piN de loh day see-gah-rait*	Have you any bread? water? cigarettes?
Est-ce que c'est bon?	*aisk' sai boN*	Is it good?
Est-ce qu'elle est gentille?	*ais-kail ai zhaN-teey*	Is she nice?
Est-ce que Monsieur Williams demeure ici?	*aisk' miss-y(ay) vil-yahms d'm(ai)r ee-see*	Does Mr. Williams live here?

COMMANDS AND REQUESTS

You may add **s'il vous plaît** *seel voo plai* (if you please) to each of the following:

Entrez	*aN-tray*	Come in. Go in
Sortez	*sor-tay*	Get out. Come out. Go out
Allez	*ah-lay*	Go. Go on. Get on with the job
Venez	*ve-nay*	Come
Venez ici	*ve-nay-zee-see*	Come here
Venez vite	*ve-nay veet*	Come quickly
Passez par là	*pah-say pahr lah*	Go through that way
Entrez par ici	*aN-tray pahr ee-see*	Come in this way
Restez	*rais-tay*	Stay where you are
Restez ici	*rais-tay-zee-see*	Stay here
Regardez	*re-gahr-day*	Look
Donnez-moi ça	*do-nay mwah sah*	Give me that

Parlez anglais	*pahr-lay-zaN-glais*	Speak English
Parlez plus lentement	*pahr-lay pl(ee) laNt-maN*	Speak more slowly
Prenez	*pre-nay*	Take that
Prenez-en deux	*pre-nay-zaN d(ay)*	Take two of them
Montrez-moi ça	*moN-tray mwah sah*	Show me that
Écoutez-moi	*ay-koo-tay mwah*	Listen to me
Attendez un moment	*ah-taN-day-zuN momaN*	Wait a moment
Attendez ici	*ah-taN-day-zee-see*	Wait here
Dites-le	*deet le*	Say it
Faites-le	*fait le*	Do it
Vite! Vite!	*veet veet*	Hurry! Hurry!
Plus vite!	*pl(ee) veet*	Faster!
Asseyez-vous	*ah-say-yay-voo*	Sit down
Levez-vous	*le-vay voo*	Get up. Stand up

'Don't'

N'entrez pas!	*naN-tray pah*	Don't go in! Don't come in!
Ne sortez pas!	*ne sor-tay pah*	Don't go out! Don't come out!

N'allez pas!	*nah-lay pah*	Don't go!
Ne venez pas!	*ne ve-nay pah*	Don't come!
Ne regardez pas!	*ne re-gahr-day pah*	Don't look!
Ne le lui donnez pas!	*ne le lwee do-nay pah*	Don't give it to him!
Ne parlez pas si vite!	*ne pahr-lay pah see veet*	Don't speak so fast!
Pas si vite!	*pah see veet*	Not so fast!
N'attendez pas!	*nah-taN-day pah*	Don't wait!
Ne faites pas ça!	*ne fait pah sah*	Don't do that!
Ne faites rien!	*ne fait ryiN*	Don't do anything!
Ne leur dites rien!	*ne l(air)r deet ryiN*	Don't tell them anything!
Ne partez pas!	*ne pahr-tay pah*	Don't go away!
Ne touchez pas!	*nee too-shay pah*	Don't touch!
Assez!	*ah-say*	Enough!

Note.—1. The negative is expressed by two words, ne (n' before a vowel) and pas. Ne is placed before the verb and pas after it. If there is no verb, pas alone is used: **pas assez** = not enough.

2. To say 'not anything' (or 'nothing'), ne is placed before the verb and rien after it. If there is no verb, rien alone is used: **rien de nouveau** = nothing new; no news.

'TO HAVE' and 'TO GO'

avoir	*ah-vwahr*	to have
j'ai	*zhay*	I have
nous avons	*noo-zah-voN*	we have
vous avez	*voo-zah-vay*	you have
il (elle) a	*eel (ail) ah*	he (she) has
ils (elles) ont	*eel (ail) zoN*	they have
J'ai ceci	*zhay se-see*	I have this. I've got this
J'ai faim	*zhay fiN*	I am hungry
J'ai soif	*zhay swahf*	I am thirsty
J'ai chaud	*zhay shoh*	I am warm
J'ai froid	*zhay frwah*	I am cold
Vous avez raison	*voo-zah-vay rai-zoN*	You are right
Il a mal	*ee-lah mahl*	He is in pain
Avez-vous compris?	*ah-vay voo koN-pree*	Have you understood?
L'avez-vou pris?	*lah-vay voo pree*	Have you taken it?

aller *ah-lay* to go

je vais	*zhe vai*	I go, am going
nous allons	*noo-zah-loN*	we go, are going
vous allez	*voo-zah-lay*	you go, are going
il (elle) va	*eel (ail) vah*	he (she) goes, is going
ils (elles) vont	*eel (ail) voN*	they go, are going
Je vais à la gare	*zhe vai-zah lah gahr*	I am going to the station
Nous allons au village	*noo-zah-loN-zoh vee-lahzh*	We are going to the village
Allez-vous le faire?	*ah-lay voo le fair*	Are you going to do it?
Il va venir	*eel vah v'neer*	He will come. He is coming
Ils vont vite	*eel voN veet*	They are going fast
Comment allez-vous?	*ko-maN-tah-lay voo*	How are you?
Je vais bien	*zhe vai byiN*	I am well
Comment va-t-il?	*ko-maN vah-teel*	How is he?
Il va bien	*eel vah byiN*	He is well
Comment ça va?	*ko-maN sah vah*	How are things? How goes it?
Ça va bien	*sah vah byiN*	I'm all right. I feel fine

'THERE IS,' 'THERE ARE'

Il y a une chambre au premier étage	*eel-yah(ee)n shaNb-roh prem-yay-ray-tahzh*	There is one room on the first floor
Il y a deux chambres au deuxième	*eel-yah d(ay) shaNb-roh d(ay)z-yaim*	There are two rooms on the second
Y a-t-il une chambre au premier?	*yah-tee-l(ee)n shaNb-roh prem-yay*	Is there a room on the first floor?

Note that il y a stands for both 'there is' and 'there are.'

'SOME,' 'ANY'

Voici du pain	*vwah-see d (ee) piN*	Here is (some) bread
Y a-t-il de la viande?	*yah-teel de lah vyaNd*	Is there any meat?
Avez-vous des ciga-rettes?	*ah-vay voo day see-gah-rait*	Have you any cig-arettes?

Voilà du chocolat, de la bière et des cigarettes	*vwah-lay d(ee) shoh-koh-lah dlah byair ay day see-gah-rait*	There is (some) chocolate, (some) beer and (some) cigarettes

Whereas in English the words in brackets can be omitted, they are required in French; du before masculine nouns, de la before feminines, des before plurals, and de l' before nouns beginning with a vowel,

After a verb used in the negative, de alone is used: Il y a du café *eel-yah d(ee) kah-fay* There is (some) coffee; but: Il n'y a pas de café *eel nyah pahd kah-fay* There is no coffee.

'MUCH,' 'LITTLE'

Il boit beaucoup de bière	*eel bwah boh-kood-byair*	He drinks a lot of beer
J'ai peu d'argent	*zhay p(ay) dahr-zhaN*	I have little money. I have not much money

Nous fumons beaucoup de cigarettes	*noo f(ee)moN boh-kood see-gah-rait*	We smoke many cigarettes
Il a mangé peu de pain	*ee-lah maN-zhay p(ay) d piN*	He has not eaten much bread
Combien d'argent avez-vous?	*koN-byiN dahr-zhaN-tah-vay voo*	How much money have you got?
Combien de cigarettes y a-t-il?	*koN-byiNd see-gah-rait yah-teel*	How many cigarettes are there?

Note that expressions of quantity are followed by **de.**

'NOBODY,' 'MORE,' 'NO MORE'

Personne	*pair-son*	Nobody
Je ne vois personne	*zhe ne vwah pair-son*	I don't see anybody
Il n'y a personne	*eel nyah pair-son*	There isn't anybody
Une autre personne	*(ee)-nohtr pair-son*	Somebody else.
		Another person

Note.—1. When **personne** is used in a sentence, **ne** is placed in front of the verb.

2. Une personne is 'a person.'

Plus de dix francs	*pl(ee) de dee fraN*	More than ten francs
Encore du pain s.v.p.	*aN-kor d(ee) paiN seel voo plai*	More bread, please
Y en a-t-il encore?	*yaN-nah-teel aN-kor*	Is there any more?
Encore un peu	*aN-ko-r(ai)N p(ay)*	A little more
Encore beaucoup	*aN-kor boh-koo*	Many (much) more
Encore une fois	*aN-ko-r(ee)n fwah*	Once more
Plus jamais	*pl(ee) zhah-mai*	Never more
Plus de potage, merci	*pl(ee) de po-tahzh mair-see*	No more soup, thank you
Je n'en ai plus	*zhe naN nai pl(ee)*	I have no more
Plus rien	*pl(ee) ryiN*	Nothing left at all
Il n'y en a plus	*eel nyaN-nah pl(ee)*	There is (are) no more

Note.—Ne proceding the verb and **plus** following it means 'no more.'

'EVER,' 'NEVER,' 'HERE,' 'THERE'

Je ne fume presque jamais	*zhe ne f(ee)m praisk' zha-mai*	I hardly ever smoke
Si jamais vous revenez ici	*see zhah-mai voo rev'-nay-zee-see*	If ever you come here again
Jamais plus	*zhah-mai pl(ee)*	Never again
Je ne l'ai jamais v⸱	*zhe ne lai zhah-mai v(ee)*	I have never seen it (him, her)
Il ne vient jamais	*eel ne vyaiN zhah-mai*	He never comes

Note.—To say 'never,' place ne before and jamais after the verb.

Venez ici	*ve-nay-zee-see*	Come here
C'est ici	*sai-tee-see*	It's here. This is the place
Il n'est pas ici	*eel nai pah-zee-see*	He isn't here
Par ici	*pah-ree-see*	This way
Le voici	*le vwah-see*	Here it (he) is
La voici	*lah vwah-see*	Here it (she) is

Les voici	*lay vwah-see*	Here they are
Me voici	*me vwah-see*	Here I am
Ici ou là?	*ee-see oo lah*	Here or there?
Qui est là?	*kee ai lah*	Who is there?
Par là	*pahr lah*	That way
Le voilà	*le vwah-lah*	There it (he) is
La voilà	*lah vwah-lah*	There it (she) is
Les voilà	*lay vwah-lah*	There they are

Note that voici can mean both 'here is' and 'here are,' voilà both 'there is' and 'there are.'

EXCLAMATIONS

See also 'Expressions of Approval and Disapproval' on page 33.

Quel beau chapeau!	*kail boh sha-poh*	What a beautiful hat!
Comme il est beau!	*kom ee-lai boh*	How beautiful it is!
Quels beaux arbres!	*kail boh-zahrbr*	What a beautiful trees!
Comme ils sont beaux!	*ko-meel soN boh*	How beautiful they are!

Quelle belle fille!	*kail bail feey*	What a beautiful girl!
Quelles belles fleurs!	*kail bail fl(ai)r*	What beautiful flowers!
Quel beau temps!	*kail boh taN*	What a lovely day!
Comme il fait chaud!	*ko-meel fai shoh*	How warm it is!
Quel sale temps!	*kail sahl taN*	What a nasty day!
Comme il fait froid!	*ko-meel fai frwah*	How cold it is!
Attention!	*ah-taNs-yoN*	Mind! Look out!
Tiens!	*tyaiN*	Hullo! Really!
Un moment!	*(ai)N moh-maN*	One moment!
Dites-donc!	*deet doNk*	I say! Listen!
Allons donc!	*ah-loN doNk*	Nonsense! Not a bit of it!
Pensez donc!	*paN-say doNk*	Just think!
Mon Dieu!	*mon dy(ay)*	Good gracious!
Hé! Holà!	*ay; o-lah*	Hallo! I say! (to call somebody's attention)

WANTS AND WISHES

Je veux partir	*zhe v(ay) pahr-teer*	I want to leave
le faire	*le fair*	do it
manger	*maN-zhay*	eat
boire	*bwahr*	drink
fumer	*f(ee)-may*	smoke
dormir	*dor-meer*	sleep
Veuillez . . .	*v(ay)-yay*	Will you please . . .
Ayez la bonté de . . .	*ay-yay lah boN-tay de*	Have the kindness to . . .
Je voudrais . . .	*zhe vood-rai*	I should like to . . .
Voulez-vous . . . ?	*voo-lay voo*	Do you want to . . . ?
Voudriez-vous . . . ?	*vood-ryai voo*	Would you like to . . . ?
Que voulez-vous?	*ke voo-lay voo*	What do you want?
Que veut-il?	*ke v(ay)-teel*	What does he want?
Il veut jouer	*eel v(ay) zhoo-ay*	He wants to play
Est-ce-que vous serez aussi gentille de . . . ?	*aisk' voo say-ray oh-see zhaN-tee de*	Would you be so kind as to . . . ?

LIKES AND DISLIKES

See also 'Expressions of Approval and Disapproval' on page 33.

Aimez-vous	*ai-may voo*	Do you like
Paris?	*pah-ree*	Paris?
la France?	*la fraNs*	France?
le vin rouge?	*le vaiN roozh*	red wine?
les poissons?	*lay pwah-soN*	fish?
le tennis?	*le tai-nees*	tennis?
les fraises?	*lay fraiz*	strawberries?
Je l'aime bien	*zhe laim byaiN*	I like it very much
Je les aime	*zhe lay-zaim*	I like them
Mieux que ...	*my(ay) ke*	Better than ...
Mais je préfère ...	*mai zhe pray-fair*	But I prefer ...
Et j'aime le mieux ...	*ay zhaim le my(ay)*	And I like ... best
Je n'aime pas ...	*zhe naim pah*	I don't like ...
Je le (les) déteste	*zhe le (lay) day-taist*	I hate it (them)

PERMISSION

Est-ce que je peux ...?	aisk' zhe p(ay)	Can I ...?
Vous pouvez	voo poo-vay	You can (may)
le prendre	le praNdr	take it
le faire	le fair	do it
venir	ve-neer	come
Je ne peux pas ...	zhe ne p(ay) pah	I cannot ...
Pouvons nous ...?	poo-voN noo	Can we ...?
Permettez-moi de ...	pair-mai-tay mwah de	Allow me to ...
Laissez-moi ...	lai-say mwah	Let me ...
Je vous en prie	zhe voo-zaN pree	By all means

NECESSITY

Faut-il attendre?	foh-teel ah-taNdr	Do I have to wait?
payer?	pai-yay	Do we have to pay?
partir?	pahr-teer	Does one have to leave?

y aller?	*ee ah-lay*	Does one have to go there?
l'attendre?	*lah-taN dr*	Does one have to wait for it (him, her)?
Est-ce nécessaire?	*ai-se nay-say-sair*	Is it necessary?
obligatoire?	*ob-lee-gaht-wahr*	compulsory?
facultatif?	*fah-k(ee)l-tah-teef*	optional?

INQUIRY AND INFORMATION

See also 'Asking One's Way' on page 111; 'Asking Questions' on pages 35 to 45.

Où puis-je avoir ...?	*oopwee zhe ahv-wahr*	Where can I get ...?
Quand puis-je avoir ...?	*kaN pwee zhe ahv-wahr*	When can I get ...?
Comment puis-je avoir ...?	*ko-maN pwee zhe ahv-wahr*	How can I get ...?

Savez-vous si ...?	sah-vay voo see	Do you know if ...?
Comment s'appelle	ko-maNh-sah-pail	What is this
cette rue?	sait r(ee)	street called?
cette gare?	sait gahr	station called?
ce village?	se vee-lahzh	village called?
Qu'y a-t-il?	kee yah-teel	What has happened?
Qu'est-ce qu'il y a?	kaiskee l yah	What is the matter?
A quoi cela sert-il?	ah kwah s'lah sair-teel	What is that for?
		What is the use of that?
Pouvez-vous me	poo-vay voo me	Can you
dire ...?	deer	tell me ...?
donner ...?	do-nay	give me ...?
recommander ...?	re-ko-maN-day	recommend me ...?
vendre ...?	vaNdr	sell me ...?
Je voudrais me ren-	zhe voo-drai me raN-	I should like to in-
seigner sur . .	sain-yay s(ee)r	quire about ...
Pourriez-vous me don-	poor-yay voo me do-	Could you give me
ner des renseigne-	nay day raN-sainay-	information
ments sur ...?	maN s(ee)r	about ...?
Le bureau de ren-	le b(ee)-roh de raN-	the inquiry-office
seignements	sainy'maN	

MEETING PEOPLE

Permettez-moi de vous présenter . . .	*pair-mai-tay mwah de voo pray-zaNtay*	Allow me to intoduce . . . to you
Veuillez me présenter à monsieur (madame)?	*v(ai)-yay me pray-zaN-tay ah mis-y(ay) (mah-dahm)*	Would you kindly introduce me to the gentleman (lady)?
Enchanté de faire votre connaissance	*aN-shaN-tay de fair votr ko-nai-saNs*	(I am) pleased to make you acquaintance
J'espère avoir le plaisir de vous revoir	*zhais-pair av-wahr le plai-zeer de voo re-vwahr*	I hope to meet you again
Monsieur . . . est-il chez lui?	*miss-y(ay) ai-teel shay lwee*	Is Mr. . . . at home?
Je reviendrai	*zhe re-vyiN-dray*	I shall call again
Qui dois-je annoncer?	*kee dwah-zhe ah-noN-say*	What name shall I say?
Donnez-vous la peine d'entrer?	*do-nay voo la pain daN-tray*	Will you come in, please?

Veuillez attendre un instant?	*v(ay)-yay zah-taNdr (ai)N-naiNs-taN*	Will you please wait a few moments?
Je viens un peu tard	*zhe vyaiN (ai)N p(ay) tahr*	I am rather late
Pas du tout	*pah d(ee) too*	Not at all
Qu'y a-t-il pour votre service?	*kyah-teel poor votr sair-vees*	What can I do for you?
Vous êtes bien aimable	*voo-zait byai-nai-mahbl*	That is very kind of you
Il est temps de vous dire au revoir	*ee-lai taN de voo deer oh r'vwahr*	I must be off now
Mes compliments à . . .	*may koN-plee-maN tah*	Kind regards to . . .
Merci, M . . ., je n'y manquerai pas	*mair-see, m . . ., zhe nee maNk'ray pah*	Thank you, I won't forget
Comment allez-vous? Comment ça va?	*ko-maN-tah-lay voo ko-maN sah vah?*	How are you?
Merci, M . . ., très bien	*mair-see, m . . ., trai byaiN*	Very well, thank you
Pas mal; et vous?	*pah mahl ay voo*	Not bad; and you?

Comment va Monsieur votre père?	*ko-maN vah miss-y(ay) votr pair*	How is your father?
Madame votre mère?	*mah-dahm votr mair*	mother?
Je suis heureux de l'apprendre	*zhe swee-z(ay)-r(ay) de lahp-raNdr*	I am pleased to hear it
Je regrette de l'apprendre	*zhe re-grait de lahp-raNdr*	I am sorry to hear it

SPEAKING AND UNDERSTANDING

Parlez-vous anglais?	*pahr-lay voo aN-glai*	Do you speak English
Un peu seulement	*(ai)N p(ay) s(ay)l'maN*	Only a little
Y a-t-il quelqu'un qui parle anglais?	*yah-teel kail-k(ai)N kee pahrl aN-glai*	Is there anybody who speaks English?
Comprenez-vous?	*koN-pre-nay voo*	Do you understand?
Je comprends si vous parlez lentement	*zhe koN praN see voo pahr-lay laNt-maN*	I understand if you speak slowly
Je ne comprends pas	*zhen'koN-praN pah*	I don't understand

Ne parlez pas si vite	ne pahr-lay pah see veet	Don't speak so fast
Comment dit-on . . . en anglais?	ko-maN-dee-toN ahnaN-glai	What is . . . in English?
Que veut dire . . . ?	ke v(ay) deer	What does . . . mean?
Veuillez répéter	v(ai)-yay ray-pay-tay	Please repeat
expliquer	aiks-plee-kay	explain
leur dire	l(ai)r deer	tell them
lui demander	lwee d'maN-day	ask him (her)

PRONOUNS AND POSSESSIVES

'ME,' 'YOU,' 'HIM,' 'HER'

Il m'attend	eel mah-taN	He is expecting (waiting for) me
Il ne m'attend pas	eel ne mah-taN pah	He is not expecting (waiting for) me
Je vous connais	zhe voo ko-nai	I know you

Je ne vous connais pas	*zhe ne voo ko-nai pah*	I don't know you
Connaissez-vous ce monsieur?	*ko-nai-say voo se mis-y(ay)*	Do you know this gentleman?
Le connaissez-vous?	*le ko-nai-say voo*	Do you know him?
Je ne le connais pas	*zhe ne le ko-nai pah*	I don't know him
La connaissez-vous?	*lah ko-nai-say voo*	Do you know her?
Je l'aime	*zhe laim*	I love him (her, it)
Elle m'aime	*ail maim*	She loves me
Je ne vous aime pas	*zhe ne voo-zaim pah*	I don't love you

Note that me (me), vous (you), le (him), la (her) precede the verb. Me, le, la are changed to m', l', l' before a vowel or *h* mute.

'IT,' 'THEM'

Voici votre verre	*vwah-see votr vair*	Here is your glass
Prenez-le!	*pre-nay le*	Take it
Voici votre tasse	*vwah-see votr tahs*	Here is your cup
Prenez-la!	*pre-nay lah*	Take it
Voilà les allumettes	*vwah-lah lay-zah-l(ee)-mait*	Here are the matches
Prenez-les!	*pre-nay lay*	Take them

Ceci est mon journal	se-see ai moN zhoor-nahl	This is my newspaper
Ne le prends pas	ne le praN pah	Don't take it
C'est ma plume	sai mah pl(ee)m	It is my pen
Ne la prends pas	ne lah praN pah	Don't take it
Ce sont mes gants	se soN may gaN	They are my gloves
Ne les prends pas	ne lay praN pah	Don't take them
Voilà le billet	vwah-la le bee-yay	There is the ticket
Le voilà	le vwah-lah	There it is
Voici les journaux	vwah-see lay zhoor-noh	Here are the newspapers
Les voici	lay vwah-see	Here they are
Voici la serveuse	vwah-see lah sair-v(ay)z	Here is the waitress
La voici	lah vwah-see	Here she is
Voilà les enfants	vwah-lah lay-zaN-faN	There are the children
Les voilà	lay vwah-lah	There they are

The personal pronouns le (him, it), la (her, it), les (them), etc., follow the verb in the Imperative, if it is in the Affirmative.

If the Imperative is in the Negative, all personal pronouns are placed between ne and the verb.

'TO HIM,' 'TO HER,' 'TO THEM'

Dites-lui . . .	*deet lwee*	Tell him . . .; Tell her . . .
Dites-leur . . .	*deet l(ai)r*	Tell them . . .
Écrivez-lui . . .	*ay-kree-vay lwee*	Write to him (her)
Parlez-leur . . .	*pahr-lay l(ai)r*	Speak to them
Demandez	*d'maN-day*	Ask
Répondez	*ray-poN-day*	Answer
Ne lui parlez pas	*ne lwee pahr-lay pah*	Don't speak to him (her)
Ne leur répondez pas	*ne l(ai)r ray poN-day pah*	Don't reply to them
Demandons-lui	*d'maN-doN lwee*	Let us ask him (her)
Leur écrivez-vous?	*l(ai)r-ay-kree-vay voo*	Are you writing to them?
Je ne leur écris pas	*zhe ne l(ai)-ray-kree pah*	I am not writing to them
Ils (elles) lui parlent	*eel (ail) lwee pahrl*	They are speaking to him (her)
Nous leur écrivons	*noo l(ai)-ray-kree-voN*	We are writing to them

In the same way as **me, le, la, les** the words **lui** (to him or to her) and **leur** (to them) precede the verb or the negative imperative.

OF THE, TO THE

La femme du pro-fesseur	*lah fam d(ee) pro-fais(air)r*	The teacher's wife
La maison de mon père	*lah may-zoN de moN pair*	My father's house
Le parapluie de la dame	*le pah-rah-plwee de lah dahm*	The lady's umbrella
Les parents des en-fants	*lay pah-raN day-zaN-fan*	The children's parents
Les souliers de l'en-fant	*lay sool-yay de laN-faN*	The child's shoes
Le nom de l'hôtel	*le noN de loh-tail*	The name of the hotel
Envoyez-le à cette adresse	*aN-vwah-yay le ah sai-tah-drais*	Send it to this address
Parlez au monsieur	*pahr-lay oh mis-y(ay)*	Speak to the gentle-man
Demandez à la dame	*d'maN-day ah lah dahm*	Ask the lady

| Répondez aux en-fants | *ray-poN-day oh-zaN-faN* | Answer the children |
| Retournons à l'hôtel | *re-toor-noN zah loh-tail* | Let us go back to the hotel |

Note.—1. 'The teacher's wife' must be turned into 'the wife of the teacher,' 'My father's house' into 'the house of my father,' etc.

2. When de or à precede le or les the following contracted forms are used:

> du instead of de le
> des ,, ,, de les
> au ,, ,, à le
> aux ,, ,, à les

No contractions are used for de la, de l', à la, à l'.

3. Whereas in English the 'to' is omitted in sentences like 'He sends the lady flowers,' it must not be left out in French. The same applies to the verbs dire (to tell), demander (to ask), répondre (to answer), and others. It is not difficult to understand why these require à (to) if we realize that they also mean 'to speak to,' 'to put a question to,' 'to reply to.'

'THIS,' 'THAT,' 'THESE,' 'THOSE'

Ce livre est très in- téressant	*se leev-rai trai-zaiN- tay-ray-saN*	This book is very interesting
Cette lettre est pour vous	*sait lait-rai poor voo*	This letter is for you
Ces enveloppes sont déchirées	*say-zaN-v'lop soN day-shee-ray*	These envelopes are torn
Ces chaises sont réservées	*say shaiz soN ray- zair-vay*	These chairs are re- served
Cet hôtel est trop cher	*sai-toh-tail ai troh shair*	This hotel is too expensive

Note from the above examples that **ce** is used with masculine nouns, **cette** with feminines, and **cet** with masculine nouns beginning with a vowel or mute *h*. The plural is **ces** in every case.

Ce livre can mean both 'this book' and 'that book,' **cet enfant** both 'this child' and 'that child,' **ces crayons** both 'these pencils' and 'those pencils.' To emphasize the distinction between 'this' and 'that,' 'those' and 'these'—**ci** or **là** are added to the noun. Compare the following:

Ce couteau-ci	*se koo-toh see*	This knife
Ce couteau-là	*se koo-toh lah*	That knife
Cette fourchette-ci	*sait foor-shait see*	This fork
Cette fourchette-là	*sait foor-shait lah*	That fork
Cet homme-ci	*sai-tom si*	This man
Cet homme-là	*sai-tom lah*	That man
Ces hommes-ci	*say-zom see*	These men
Ces hommes-là	*say-zom lah*	Those men

If 'this' and 'that,' 'these' and 'those' are used by themselves, i.e. not in connection with nouns, special forms are used as given in the following examples:

Ceci est pour moi	*se-see ai poor mwah*	This is for me
Cela est pour vous	*se-lah ai poor voo*	That is for you
Ceux-ci sont pour lui	*s(ay)-see soN poor lwee*	These (m.) are for him
Celles-ci sont pour elle	*sail see soN poor ail*	These (f.) are for her
Ceux-là sont pour nous	*s(ay)lah soN poor noo*	Those (m.) are for us
Celles-là sont pour nous	*sail lah soN poor noo*	Those (f.) are for us

'MY,' 'YOUR,' 'HIS,' 'HER,' etc.

Mon frère	*moN frair*	My brother
Ma sœur	*ma s(ai)r*	My sister
Mon oncle	*mo-noNkl*	My uncle
Mes parents	*may pah-raN*	My parents; my relatives
Mon chapeau	*moN-shah-poh*	My hat
Ma canne	*mah kahn*	My walking stick
Mes gants	*may gaN*	My gloves
Son père	*soN pair*	His or her father
Sa mère	*sah mair*	His or her mother
Ses enfants	*say-zaN-faN*	His or her children
Son argent	*soN-nahr-zhaN*	His or her money
Ses livres	*say leevr*	His or her books
Votre tante	*votr taNt*	Your aunt
Votre stylo	*votr stee-loh*	Your fountain-pen
Vos cigarettes	*voh-see-gah-rait*	Your cigarettes
Notre jardin	*notr zhar-daiN*	Our garden
Nos enfants	*noh-zaN-faN*	Our children
Leur cousin	*l(ai)r koo-zaiN*	Their cousin
Leurs petits-enfants	*l(ai)r p'tee-zaN-faN*	Their grandchildren

The possessive adjectives (my, your, his, etc.), like any other adjectives in French, agree in gender with the thing possessed. **Son chapeau** is both 'His hat' and 'Her hat,' because **chapeau** is masculine in French; **sa tasse** stands for both 'his' and 'her cup,' as **tasse** is feminine in French.

'MINE,' 'YOURS,' 'HIS,' 'HERS', etc.

Ceci est à moi	*se-see ai-tah mwah*	This is mine
Cela est à vous	*se-lah ai-tah voo*	That is yours
Ceux-ci sont à lui	*s(ay)-see soN-tah lwee*	These (m.) are his
Celles-ci sont à elle	*sail see soN-tah ail*	These (f.) are hers
Ceux-là sont à nous	*s(ay) lah soN-tah noo*	Those (m.) are ours
Celles-là sont à eux	*sail lah soN-tah (aỳ)*	Those (f.) are theirs (m.)
Ceci est à elles	*se-see ai-tah ail*	This is theirs (f.)

'MYSELF,' 'YOURSELF,' 'HIMSELF,' etc.

Je le ferai moi-même	*zhe le fe-ray mwah maim*	I shall do it myself
Le ferez-vous vous-même	*le fe-ray voo voo maim*	Will you do it yourself?
Il le fera lui-même	*eel le fe-rah lwee maim*	He will do it himself

Elle le fera elle-même	*ail le fe-rah ail maim*	She will do it herself
Nous le ferons nous-mêmes	*noo le fe-roN noo maim*	We shall do it our-selves

'TO BE,' AND 'TO DO'

'ISN'T IT?' 'DON'T YOU?' 'AREN'T YOU?' 'ISN'T HE?' 'DOESN'T SHE?' etc.

Vous êtes Francais, n'est-ce pas?	*voo-zait fraN-sai nais pah*	You are French, aren't you?
Vous parlez anglais, n'est-ce pas?	*voo pahr-lay-zaN-glai nais pah*	You speak English, don't you?
C'est joli, n'est-ce pas?	*sai zho-lee nais pah*	It is pretty, isn't it?
Vous venez ce soir, n'est-ce pas?	*voo v'nay se swahr nais pah*	You'll come this evening, won't you?

Note.—N'est-ce pas? is short for N'est-ce pas vrai? = Is it not true?

IT IS ... IT WAS ..

1. C'est bon   *sai   boN*   It is   good
   C'était bien   *say-tai byaiN*   It was all right
         facile   *fah-seel*   easy
         difficile   *dee-fee-seel*   difficult
         vrai   *vrai*   true
         curieux   *k(ee)r-y(ay)*   strange
         drôle   *drohl*   funny
         amusant   *ah-m(ee)-zaN*   amusing
         mon pro-   *moN proh-fais-*   my teacher
         fesseur   *s(ai)r*

Est-ce votre sac?   *ai-se votr sahk*   Is it your handbag?
Était-ce votre   *ay-tai se votr shaiz*   Was it your chair?
   chaise?

Note.—'It is' = C'est if followed by a noun, or by an adjective, provided
the word 'it' does not replace a noun (as in the following examples).

2. Le verre—il est   *le vair ee-lai kah-say*   The glass—it is broken
         cassé

| | il était
cassé | *ee-lay-tai kah-
say* | it was broken |

Note.—'It is' = il est when 'it' replaces a masculine noun.

3. La clé—elle est
   perdue
   elle était
   perdue | *la klay ai-lai pair-
d(ee)*
*ai-lay-tai pair-
d(ee)* | The key—it is lost
it was lost

Note.—'It is' = elle est when 'it' replaces a feminine noun.

4. Il est six heures
   Il était midi
   tard
   presque
   minuit | *ee-lai see-z(ai)r*
ee-lay-tai mee-dee
tahr
*praisk' meen-
wee* | It is six o'clock
It was noon
late
nearly mid-
night

Note.—'It is' = il est when speaking of time.

5. Il fait beau
   Il faisait mauvais
   chaud
   froid
   du vent | *eel fai boh*
eel fe-zai moh-vai
shoh
frwah
d(ee) vaN | It is fine
It was nasty
hot
cold
windy

Note.—'It is' = il fait when speaking of the weather.

6. Il pleut	*eel pl(ay)*	It is raining
neige	*naizh*	snowing
gèle	*zhail*	freezing
dégèle	*day-zhail*	thawing
Il pleuvait	*eel pl(ay)-vai*	It was raining
neigeait	*nai-zhai*	snowing
gelait	*zhe-lai*	freezing
dégelait	*day-zhe-lai*	thawing

'Did you ...?' 'I didn't ...'

1. Avez-vous com- mencé?	*ah-vay voo ko-manN- say*	Did you start?
Je n'ai pas fini	*zh'nay pah fee-nee*	I didn't finish
mange	*maN-zhay*	eat
payé	*pai-yay*	pay
L'avez vous pris	*la-vay voo pree*	Did you take it?
Je ne l'ai pas fait	*zhe ne lay pah fai*	I didn't do it
trouvé	*troo-vay*	find it
acheté	*ahsh-tay*	buy it
payé	*pai-yay*	pay for it
2. Êtes-vous allé?	*ait vooz-ah-lay*	Did you go?

Je ne suis pas venu sorti parti	zhen'swee pah ve-n(ee) sort-ee pahr-tee	I didn't come go out leave
Je suis allé chez le coiffeur	zhe swee-zah-lay shay le kwah-f(ai)r	I went to the hair-dresser's
Je suis venu hier soir	zhe swee ve-n(ee) yair swahr	I came last night
Elle est sortie après le déjeuner	ai-lai sortee ahp-rai le day-zh(ai)-nay	She went out after lunch
Ils sont partis de bonne heure	eel soN pahr-tee de bo-n(ai)r	They left early
3. Vous êtes-vous coupé?	voo-zait voo koo-pay	Did you cut yourself?
Je ne me suis pas brûlé	zhen' me swee pah br (ee)-lay	I didn't burn myself
Je ne me suis pas fait mal	zhen' me swee pah fai mahl	I didn't hurt myself
Je ne me suis pas amusé	zhen' me swee pah zah-m(ee)-zay	I didn't enjoy myself

Note.—1. Avez-vous . . .? is the usual translation for 'Did you?' Je n'ai pas . . . for 'I didn't.'

2. Etes-vous...? Je ne suis pas... are used with verbs denoting movement from one place to another (to come, to go, to climb, to fall, etc.).

3. Vous êtes-vous...? Je ne me suis pas... are used with reflexive verbs, i.e. verbs where the action is done by yourself and to yourself.

'I SHALL...,' 'WILL YOU?'

1. Je vais sortir jouer?	*zhe vai sor-teer* *zhoo-ay*	I am going to go out (I shall) play
Allez-vous l'acheter?	*ah-lay voo lashh-tay*	Are you going to buy it?
le faire?	*le fair*	(Will you) do it?
le chercher?	*le shair-shay*	fetch it?
les voir?	*lay vwahr*	see them?
Il va vous en acheter	*eel vah voo-zaN- nahsh-tay*	He is going to buy you some
Nous allons la chercher	*noo-zah-loN lah shair- shay*	We are going to look for her
Ils vont partir	*eel voN pahr-teer*	They are going to leave
2. Je partirai demain	*zhe pahr-tee-ray de- maiN*	I shall leave to- morrow

Irez-vous aussi?	*ee-ray voo-zoh-see*	Will you go too?
Il viendra mardi	*eel vyaiN-drah mahr-dee*	He will come on Tuesday
Nous irons à pied	*noo-zee-roN-zah pyay*	We shall go on foot
Ils ne viendront pas	*eel ne vyaiN-droN pah*	They will not come

Note.—1. The immediate future is expressed by **je vais**, 'I am going to.'
2. The future tense of verbs is expressed by endings added to the verb, and not as in English by special words (shall, will).

NUMBERS

0	zéro	*zay-roh*	7	sept	*sait*
1	un	*(ai)N*	8	huit	*weet*
2	deux	*d(ay)*	9	neuf	*n(ai)f*
3	trois	*trwah*	10	dix	*dees*
4	quatre	*kahtr*	11	onze	*oNz*
5	cinq	*saiNk*	12	douze	*dooz*
6	six	*sees*	13	treize	*traiz*

14	quatorze	*ka-torz*	18	dix-huit	*dee-zweet*
15	quinze	*kaiNz*	19	dix-neuf	*deez n(ai)f*
16	seize	*saiz*	20	vingt	*vaiN*
17	dix-sept	*dee sait*	21	vingt-et-un	*vaiN-tay uN*

22	vingt-deux	*vaiN d(ay)*
23	vingt-trois	*vaiN trwah*
30	trente	*traNt*
31	trente-et-un	*traN-tay uN*
32	trente-deux	*traN d(ay)*
40	quarante	*kah-raNt*
50	cinquante	*saiN-kaNt*
60	soixante	*swah-saNt*
70	soixante-dix	*swah-saNt dees*
71	soixante-et-onze	*swah-saNt oNz*
72	soixante-douze	*swah-saNt dooz*
73	soixante-treize	*swah-saNt traiz*
79	soixante-dix-neuf	*swah-saNt deez n(ai)f*
80	quatre-vingts	*kahtr vaiN*
90	quatre-vingt-dix	*kahtr vaiN dees*
91	quatre-vingt-onze	*kahtr vaiN toNz*
92	quatre-vingt-douze	*kahtr vaiN dooz*
100	cent	*saN*

200	deux cents	*d(ay) saN*
1,000	mille	*meel*
in 1973	en dix-neuf cent soixante-treize	*aN deez n(ai)f saN swah-saN-traiz*

1st	premier, première	*prem-yay prem-yair*
2nd	second, seconde or deuxième	*zgoN zgoNd d(ay)z-yaim*
3rd	troisième	*trwahz-yaim*
4th	quatrième	*kahtr-yaim*
5th	cinquième	*saiNk-yaim*
6th	sixième	*seez-yaim*
7th	septième	*sait-yaim*
8th	huitième	*weet-yaim*
9th	neuvième	*n(ai)v-yaim*
10th	dixième	*deez-yaim*

Note.—The first of a month is le premier, but the second, third, etc. le deux, le trois, etc. (see page 102).

WEIGHTS AND MEASURES

un kilogramme or kilo = 1,000 grammes = 2·2 lb.　　*(ai)N kee-loh-grahm kee-loh meel grahm*

un demi-kilo or une livre = 500 grammes = 1·1 lb.　　*(ai)N d'mee kee-loh (ee)n leevr*

un quintal métrique = 100 kilos = 2 cwt.　　*(ai)N kiN-tahl mayt-reek*

1 ounce = 28 grammes; 1 pound = 453 grammes; 1 cwt. = 508 kilos

lourd	*loor*	heavy
léger	*lay-zhay*	light
peser	*pe-zay*	to weigh
le poids	*pwah*	the weight
une balance	*(ee)n bah-laNs*	scales

1 mètre = 100 centimètres = 1,000 millimètres = 39 inches　　*(ai)N maitr saN saN-tee-maitr meel mee-lee-maitr*

1 centimètre = 10 millimètres = ⅖ inch (approx.)　　*(ai)N saN-tee-maitr dee mee-lee-maitr*

1 kilomètre = 1,000 mètres = ⅝ of a mile　　*(ai)N kee-loh-màitr meel maitr*

1 inch = 2½ centimètres; 1 foot = 30 centimètres (approx.)

1 yard = 90 centimètres (approx.); 5 miles = 8 kilomètres (approx.)

long (court)	*loN (koor)*	long (short)
large (étroit)	*lahrzh (ay-trwah)*	wide (narrow)
haut (profond)	*oh (pro-foN)*	high (deep)
cinq mètres de long sur trois mètres de large	*SaiNK maitr de loN s(ee)r trwah maitr de lahrzh*	5 metres long by 3 metres wide

1 litre	*leetr*	= 1¾ pints	1 pint	=	(approx.)	½ litre
2 litres		= 3½ pints	1 quart	=	,,	1 litre
5 litres		= 1 gallon ¾ pints	1 gallon	=	,,	4½ litres

NOTICES

Entrée	Entrance
Sortie	Exit
Ouvert	Open
Fermé	Shut
Fumeurs	Smokers
Non-fumeurs	Non-smokers
Poussez	Push
Tirez	Pull

Défense de fumer	Smoking prohibited
Défense de cracher	Do not spit
Défense d'afficher	Billposting prohibited
Cabinet	Lavatory
Occupé	Engaged
Libre	Free
Chaud	Hot
Froid	Cold
Entrée interdite au public	No admittance
A vendre	For sale
A louer	To let
Entrez sans frapper	Walk in without knocking
Tournez le bouton s.v.p.	Please turn the handle
Essuyez vos pieds, s.v.p.	Please wipe your feet
Arrêt fixe	Bus stop
Arrêt facultatif	Stop by request
Prenez garde à la peinture	Wet paint
Tenir les chiens en laisse	Dogs must be led
Sens interdit	No entry
Sens unique	One-way street
Rue barrée	No thoroughfare
Attention Travaux!	Road Works Ahead!

FOOD AND DRINK

The following list is arranged alphabetically to enable a better understanding of French menus. If the name of a dish is not found under the first word, it should be looked up under the second, e.g. 'supreme de poulet' under 'poulet.'

abattis (m.pl.)	*ah-bah-tee*	giblets
ablette (f.)	*ah-blait*	bleak
abricots (m.pl.)	*ah-bree-koh*	apricots
agneau (m.)	*ahn-yoh*	lamb
aiglefin (m.)	*aigl-faiN*	haddock
ail (m.)	*ahy*	garlic
aile (f.)	*ail*	wing of poultry
aloyau (m.)	*al-wah-yoh*	sirloin (of beef)
amande (f.)	*ah-maNd*	almond
anchois (m.)	*aN-shwah*	anchovy
andouille (f.)	*aN-dooy*	chitterlings made into sausages
anguille (f.)	*aN-geey*	eel

ananas (m.)	*ah-nah-nahs*	pineapple
artichauds (m.pl.)	*ahr-tee-shoh*	artichokes
asperge (f.)	*ahs-pairzh*	asparagus
assiette assortie	*ahs-yai-tah-sor-tee*	assortment of cold tongue, ham and beef
aubergine (f.)	*oh-bair-zheen*	fruit of the egg plant
baba (m.)	*bah-bah*	kind of sponge cake steeped in rum syrup
banane (f.)	*bah-nahn*	banana
barbue (f.)	*bahr-(bee)*	brill
bécasse (f.)	*bay-kahs*	woodcock
bécassine (f.)	*bay-kah-seen*	snipe
beignets (m.pl.)	*bain-yay*	fritters
betterave (f.)	*bait'rahv*	beetroot
beurre (m.)	*b(ai)r*	butter
au beurre	*oh b(ai)r*	cooked in butter
au beurre noir	*oh (b(ai)r nwahr*	with browned butter sauce
bifteck (m.)	*beef-taik*	beefsteak
aux pommes	*oh pom*	steak and chips

bisque (f.)	*beesk*	shell-fish soup
blanc-manger (m.)	*blaN-maN-zhay*	blancmange
blanquette (f.)	*blaN-kait*	stew of veal with sauce
bœuf (m.)	*b(ai)f*	beef
à la mode	*ah lah mod*	stewed beef
bombe glacée	*boNb glah-say*	ice pudding
bouchée (f.)	*boo-shay*	pie or patty,
à la reine	*ah lah rain*	poultry pie
boudin (m.)	*boo-daiN*	black pudding
bouillabaise (f.)	*boo-yah-bais*	soup or stew of fish with tomatoes, onions and garlic
bouilli (m.)	*boo-yee*	boiled (beef)
bouillie (f.)	*boo-yee*	gruel, porridge
bouillon (m.)	*boo-yoN*	meat soup; beef tea
boulette (f.)	*boo-lait*	meat ball, rissole
brochet (m.)	*bro-shai*	pike
brugnon (m.)	*br(ee)n-yoN*	nectarine
cabillaud (m.)	*kah-bee-yoh*	codfish; fresh cod
caille (f.)	*kahy*	quail
canard (m.)	*kah-nahr*	duck

canard sauvage (m)	*kah-nahr so-vazh*	wild duck
caneton (m.)	*kahn-toN*	duckling
cannelle (f.)	*kah-nail*	cinnamon
câpre (f.)	*kahpr*	caper
caramel (m.)	*kah-rah-mail*	burnt sugar
carottes (f.pl.)	*kah-rot*	carrots
carpe (f.)	*kahrp*	carp
carrelet (m.)	*kahr-lay*	plaice
casse croûte (m.)	*kas-kroot*	snack
cassis (m.)	*kah-see*	black currant
céleri (m.)	*sayl-ree*	celery
cerfeuil (m.)	*sair-f(ai)y*	chervil
cerise (f.)	*s'reez*	cherry
cervelas (m.)	*sair-velah*	saveloy
cervelle (f.) de veau	*sair-vail (de voh)*	(calves') brains
champignons (m.pl.)	*shaN-peen-yoN*	mushrooms
chapon (m.)	*shah-poN*	capon
charlotte (f.)	*shahr-lot*	apple charlotte; trifle
châteaubriant (m.)	*shah-toh-bree-aN*	grilled steak
châtaigne (f.)	*shah-tainy*	chestnut
chevreuil (m.)	*shev-r(ai)y*	venison
chicorée (f.)	*shee-koh-ray*	chicory

chicorée frisée	*shee-koh-ray free-zay*	endive
chou (m.)	*shoo*	cabbage
de Bruxelles	*shoo de br(ee)-sail*	Brussels sprouts
frisé	*'shoo free-zay*	kale
de Milan	*shoo de mee-laN*	Savoy cabbage
à la crème	*shoo ah lah kraim*	cream bun
choucroute (f.)	*shoo-kroot*	sauerkraut
chou-fleur (m.)	*shoo-fl(ai)r*	cauliflower
chou-rave (m.)	*shoo-rahv*	kohlrabi
ciboulette (f.)	*see-boo-lait*	chive
citron (m.)	*seet-roN*	lemon
citrouille (f.)	*seet-rooy*	pumpkin
civet (m.)	*see-vai*	stew (of venison, etc.)
civet de lièvre	*see-vai de lyaivr*	jugged hare
clou (m.) de girofle	*kloo de zhee-rofl*	clove
cochon de lait (m.)	*koh-shoN de lai*	sucking pig
en cocotte (f.)	*koh-kot*	cooked with bacon in stew-pan
cœurs (m.pl.)	*k(ai)r*	hearts
de laitue	*de lai-t(ee)*	of lettuce
de filet	*de fee-lay*	tender loin steak
coings (m.pl.)	*kwaiN*	quince

compote (f.)	*koN-pot*	stewed fruit
concombre (m.)	*koN-koNbr*	cucumber
condiments (m.pl.)	*koN-dee-maN*	seasoning
confitures (f.pl.)	*koN-fee-t(ee)r*	preserves; jam
conserve (f.)	*koN-sairv*	preserved food
conserves au vinaigre	*koN-sairv oh vee-naigr*	pickles
conserves en boîtes	*aN bwaht*	tined food
bœuf de conserve	*b(ai)f de koN-sairv*	corned beef
consommé (m.)	*koN-so-may*	clear soup; stock
coq (m.)	*kok*	cock
d'Inde	*kok daiN-d*	turkey cock
de bruyère	*kok de br(ee)-yair*	grouse
coquillage (m.)	*ko-kee-yahzh*	shell-fish
cornichon (m.)	*kor-nee-shoN*	gherkin
côtelette (f.)	*koht-lait*	cutlet; chop
courge (f.) à la moelle	*koorzh ah lah mwahl*	vegetable marrow
crabe (m.)	*krahb*	crab
crème (f.)	*kraim*	cream
crème fouettèe	*kraim foo-ai-tay*	whipped cream
crème au caramel	*kraim oh ka-ra-mail*	caramel custard
crêpe (f.)	*kraip*	pancake

cresson (m.)	*krai-soN*	cress
de fontaine	*de foN-tain*	watercress
crevettes (f.pl.)	*kre-vait*	shrimps
croûte (f.)	*kroot*	crust
au pot	*oh poh*	clear soup with pieces of toast
aux champignons	*oh shaN-pee-nyoN*	mushrooms on toast
cru	*kr(ee)*	raw
cuit	*kwee*	cooked
dattes (f.pl.)	*daht*	dates
daube (f.)	*dohb*	stew
dinde (f.)	*daiNd*	turkey
dindon (m.)	*daiN-doN*	turkey cock
dindonneau (m.)	*daiN-do-noh*	young turkey
échalote (f.)	*ay-shah-lot*	shallot
écrevisse (f.)	*ay-kre-vees*	(fresh-water) crayfish
endive (f.)	*aN-deev*	chicory
épaule (f.)	*ay-pol*	shoulder
éperlan (m.)	*ay-pair-laN*	smelt
épice (f.)	*ay-pees*	spice
pain d'épice	*paiN day-pees*	gingerbread
épinard (m.)	*ay-pee-nahr*	spinach

escalope (f.)	*ais-kah-lop*	cutlet (of veal)
escargot (m.)	*ais-kahr-goh*	snail
escarole (f.)	*ais-kah-rol*	endive
esturgeon (m.)	*ais-t(ee)r-zhoN*	sturgeon
étuvé	*ay-t(ee)-vay*	stewed
faisan (m.)	*fai-zaN*	pheasant
faisandé	*fai-zaN-day*	high, gamy
farce (f.)	*fahrs*	stuffing
farci	*fahr-see*	stuffed
fève (f.)	*faiv*	bean
figues (f.pl.)	*feeg*	figs
filet (m.)	*fee-lai*	fillet
faux-filet	*foh fee-lai*	sirloin
flageolet (m.)	*flah-zho-lai*	small kidney beans
foie (m.)	*fwah*	liver
four (m.)	*foor*	oven
au four	*oh foor*	baked
petits fours	*pe-tee foor*	fancy biscuits
fraise (f.)	*fraiz*	strawberry
des bois	*fraiz day bwah*	wild strawberry
framboise (f.)	*fraN-bwahz*	raspberry

friandise (f.)	*free-aN-deez*	delicacy; tit-bit
fricandeau (m.)	*free-kaN-doh*	stew of larded veal
fricassée (f.)	*free-kah-say*	fricassee
frit(e)	*free*(t)	fried
friture (f.)	*free-t(ee)r*	dish of small fried fish
fromage (m.)	*fro-mahzh*	cheese
de cochon d'Italie	*fro-mahzh de koh-shoN dee-tah-lee*	pork brawn
fruits (m.pl.)	*frwee*	fruit
fumé(e)	*f(ee)-may*	smoked
galantine (f.)	*gah-laN-teen*	galantine
galette (f.)	*gah-lait*	kind of flat cake
aux pommes	*gah-lait oh pom*	apple-tart
garbure (f.)	*gahr-b(ee)r*	mixed vegetable soup
gâteau (m.)	*gah-toh*	cake
gaufre (f.)	*gohfr*	waffle
gaufrette (f.)	*gof-rait*	wafer biscuit
gelée (f.)	*zhe-lay*	jelly
gelinotte (f.)	*zhe-lee-not*	hazel-hen
gibelotte (f.)	*zheeb-lot*	fricassee of hare or rabbit

gibier (m.)	*zheeb-yay*	game
gigot (m.)	*zhee-goh*	leg of mutton
gigue (f.)	*zheeg*	haunch (of venison)
glace (f.)	*glahs*	ice-cream
napolitaine	*nah-poh-lee-tain*	in layers of various flavours
pistache	*pees-tash*	pistachio nut (See also **vanille panaché**)
goujon (m.)	*goo-zhoN*	gudgeon
graisse (f.)	*grais*	fat
de rognon	*de roh-nyoN*	suet
de rôti	*roh-tee*	dripping
de porc	*por*	lard
gras, grasse	*grah, grahs*	fat, rich
gras double (m.)	*grah doobl*	tripe
grenade (f.)	*gre-nahd*	pomegranate
grillade (f.)	*gree-yahd*	grilled meat
grive (f.)	*greev*	thrush
groseille (f.)	*gro-zaiy*	currant
à maquereau	*ah ma-ke-roh*	gooseberry

gruau (m.)	*gr(ee)-oh*	gruel
d'avoine	*dahv-wahn*	oatmeal
hachis (m.)	*ah-shee*	minced meat
hareng (m.)	*ah-raN*	herring
bouffi	*boo-fee*	bloater
fumé	*f(ee)-may*	kipper
haricots verts (m.pl.)	*ah-ree-koh vair*	French beans
d'Espagne	*dais-pany*	scarlet runners
beurre	*b(ai)r*	butter beans
homard (m.)	*o-mahr*	lobster
hors d'œuvre (m.)	*or-d(ai)vr*	hors-d'oeuvre
huile (f.)	*(w)eel*	oil
huîtres (f.)	*(w)eetr*	oysters
hure (m.)	*(ee)r*	boar's head
jambon (m.)	*zhaN-boN*	ham
jambonneau (m.)	*zhaN-bo-noh*	knuckle of ham
jardinière (f.)	*zhar-dee-nee-air*	with mixed vegetables
julienne (f.)	*zh(ee)l-yain*	clear soup with shredded vegetables
laitue (f.)	*lai-t(ee)*	lettuce
langouste (f.)	*laN-goost*	crayfish

langue (f.)	*laNg*	tongue
lapin (m.)	*lah-piN*	rabbit
lard (m.)	*lahr*	bacon
larde (f,)	*lahrd*	larded joint
légume (m.)	*lay-g(ee)m*	vegetable
légumes verts	*vair*	greens
lentilles (f.pl.)	*laN-teey*	lentils
lièvre (m.)	*lyaivr*	hare
longe (f.)	*loNzh*	loin (of veal or venison)
macaroni (m.)	*mah-kah-roh-nee*	macaroni
macédoine (f.)	*mah-say-dwahn*	hotchpotch
de fruits	*de frwee*	fruit salad
mâche (f.)	*mahsh*	corn salad
maigre	*maigr*	lean
maïs (m.)	*mah-ees*	maize
maître d'hôtel	*maitr doh-tail*	melted butter with parsley and lemon juice
mandarine (f.)	*maN-dah-reen*	tangerine
maquereau (m.)	*mahk-roh*	mackerel
margarine (f.)	*mahr-gah-reen*	margarine

marîné	*mah-ree-nay*	pickled, soused
marmelade (f.)	*mahr-me-lahd*	marmalade, stewed fruit
marrons (m.pl.)	*mah-roN*	chestnuts
matelote (f.)	*maht-lot*	fish stew
mélange (m.)	*may-laNzh*	mixture, especially of stewed fruit
melon (m.)	*me-loN*	melon
merlan (m.)	*mair-laN*	whiting
merluche (f.)	*mair-l(ee)sh*	hake, dried cod
miel (m)	*myail*	honey
mirabelles (f.pl.)	*mee-rah-bail*	mirabelle plums
miroton (m.)	*mee-roh-toN*	stew with onion sauce
moelle (f.)	*mwahl*	marrow (of bone)
morilles (f.pl.)	*mo-reey*	morel
morue (f.)	*mo-r(ee)*	cod
moules (f.pl.)	*mool*	mussels
mousse (f.) au chocolat	*moos oh sho-koh-lah*	whipped chocolate cream
moutarde (f.)	*moo-tahrd*	mustard
mouton (m.)	*moo-toN*	mutton

mûres (f.pl.)	*m(ee)r*	mulberries
sauvages	*soh-vazh*	blackberries
myrtilles (f.pl.)	*meer-teey*	bilberries
navarin (m.)	*nah-vah-raiN*	mutton stew with
navets (m.pl.)	*nah-vai*	turnips
de Suède	*de s(w)aid*	swedes
noisette (f.)	*nwah-zait*	hazel-nut
noix (f.)	*nwah*	nut
du Brésil	*d(ee) bray-zeel* ⎫	Brazil nut
d'Amérique	*dah-may-reek* ⎭	
de coco	*de ko-ko*	coconut
de terre	*de tair*	ground nut
nouilles (f.pl.)	*noo-eey*	noodles
œuf (m.)	*(ai)f*	egg
œufs (m.pl.)	*(ay)*	eggs
œuf sur le plat	*(ai)f s(ee)r le plah*	fried egg
à la coque	*ah lah cok*	boiled egg
mollet	*moh-lay*	soft boiled egg
dur	*d(ee)r*	hard boiled egg
poché	*poh-shay*	poached egg

brouillé	*broo-yay*	scrambled egg
œufs au lait	*oh lai*	custard
œuf à la neige	*ah lah naiz*	floating islands
oie (f.)	*wah*	goose
oignons (m.pl.)	*on-yoN*	onions
omelette (f.)	*om-lait*	omelette
naturelle	*nah-t(ee)rel*	plain omelette
aux fines herbes	*oh fin-zairb*	savoury omelette
aux confitures	*oh koN-fee-t(ee)r*	sweet omelette
orange (f.)	*oh-raNzh*	orange
orange amère	*ah-mair*	bitter (Seville) orange
orangeat (m.)	*oh-raN-zhah*	candied orange peel
oseille (f.)	*oh-zaiy*	sorrel
pain (m.)	*piN*	bread
grillé	*gree-yay*	toast
frais	*frai*	new bread
rassis	*rah-see*	stale bread
d'épice	*day-pees*	ginger bread
petit pain	*pe-tee piN*	roll
panaché	*pah-nah-shay*	mixed (salad or ice-cream)

pâté (m.)	*pah-tay*	pie
pâté de cochon	*de koh-shoN*	brawn
pâté de foie gras	*de fwah grah*	goose liver paste
pâtisserie (f.)	*pah-tees-ree*	pastry
pêche (f.)	*paish*	peach
perche (f.)	*pairsh*	perch
perdreau (m.)	*pair-droh*	young partridge
perdrix (f.)	*pair-dree*	partridge
persil (m.)	*pair-see*	parsley
pet de nonne (m.)	*pai-de non*	fritter
petit suisse	*p'tee swees*	small cream cheese
pied (m.)	*pyay*	foot
pieds de cochon	*de koh-shoN*	pigs' trotters
pigeon (m.)	*pee-zhoN*	pigeon
pigeonnau (m.)	*pee-zho-noh*	young pigeon
piment (m.)	*pee-maN*	red pepper
pintade (f.)	*piN-tahd*	guinea fowl
poire (f.)	*pwahr*	pear
poireau (m.)	*pwahr-roh*	leek
pois (m.)	*pwah*	pea
petits pois	*p'-tee pwah*	green peas thick pea
purée de pois	*p(ee)-ray de pwah*	soup, pease pudding

poisson (m.)	*pwah-soN*	fish
d'eau douce	*doh-doos*	fresh-water fish
de mer	*de mair*	salt-water fish
au bleu	*oh bl(ay)*	cooked in wine
poitrine (f.)	*pwaht-reen*	breast (of veal); brisket (of beef)
poivre (m.)	*pwahvr*	pepper
pomme (f.)	*pom*	apple
pomme de terre	*de tair*	potato
pommes natures	*nah-t(ee)r*	boiled potatoes
pommes frites	*freet*	fried potatoes
purée de pommes	*p(ee)-ray de pom*	mashed potatoes
pommes de terre en robe de chambre	*pom de tair aN rob de shaNbr*	potatoes in their jackets
porc (m.)	*por*	pork
pot-au-feu (m.)	*po-toh-f(ay)*	beef broth; boiled beef with vegetables
potage (m.)	*po-tahzh*	soup
printanier	*priN-tah-nyai*	vegetable soup
potiron (m.)	*po-tee-roN*	pumpkin
pouding	$\left\{ \begin{array}{l} \textit{poo-daiN} \\ \textit{poo-ding} \end{array} \right\}$	pudding

poularde (f.)	*poo-lahrd*	fattened pullet
poule (f.)	*pool*	hen, fowl
poulet (m.)	*poo-lai*	chicken
poussin (m.)	*poo-siN*	spring chicken
pré-salé (m.)	*pray sah-lay*	salt meadow mutton
prune (f.)	*pr(en)n*	plum
de Damas	*de dah-mas*	damson
pruneau (m.)	*pr(ee)-noh*	prune
purée (f.)	*p(ee)ray*	thick sieved soup;
de pois	*de pwah*	mash pease pudding;
de pommes de terre	*de pom de tair*	mashed potatoes
radis (m.)	*rah-dee*	radish
ragoût (m.)	*rah-goo*	stew
raifort (m.)	*rai-for*	horseradish
raisins (m.pl.)	*rai-zaiN*	grapes
une grappe de	*(ee)n grap de*	bunch of grapes
raisins	*rai-zaiN*	
raisins secs	*rai-ziN saik*	raisins
raisins de Corinthe	*de koh-raiNt*	dried currants
raisins de Smyrne	*de smeern*	sultanas
rata (m.) aux choux	*rah-tah oh shoo*	bubble and squeak

reines-claude (f.pl.)	*rain-klohd*	greengages
rémoulade (f.)	*ray-moo-lahd*	a sharp sauce
rhubarbe (f.)	*r(ee)-barb*	rhubarb
ris (m.) de veau	*ree de voh*	sweetbread (veal)
riz (m.)	*ree*	rice
au lait	*oh lai*	rice pudding
rognon (m.)	*ron-yoN*	kidney
romaine (f.)	*ro-main*	cos lettuce
romsteck (m.)	*rom-staik*	rump steak
rôti (m.)	*roh-tee*	roast meat
roulade (f.)	*roo-lahd*	beef olive
saignant	*sain-yaN*	underdone
saindoux (m.)	*saiN-doo*	lard
salade (f.)	*sah-lahd*	salad
salade russe	*r(ee)s*	Russian salad
faire la salade	*fair lah sah-lahd*	to mix the salad
salé	*sah-lay*	salted
petit salé	*pe-tee sah-lay*	pickled pork
salmis (m.)	*sahl-mee*	stew of roasted game
sandwich (m.)	*saNd-witsh*	sandwich
sanglier (m.)	*saN-glee-ay*	wild boar

sauce (f.)	*sohs*	sauce
blanche	*blaNsh*	white sauce; melted butter
piquante	*pee-kaNt*	sharp sauce
tartare	*tar-tar*	sharp mayonnaise
(See also maître d'hôtel)		sauce
saucisses (f.pl.)	*soh-sees*	sausages
saucisson (m.)	*soh-see-soN*	(large "dry") sausage
sauge (f.)	*sohzh*	sage
saumon (m.)	*soh-moN*	salmon
savarin (m.)	*sah-vah-riN*	kind of cake steeped in rum
sel (m.)	*sail*	salt
selle (f.) de mouton	*sail de moo-toN*	saddle of mutton
semoule (f.)	*s'mool*	semolina
sole (f.)	*sol*	sole
soupe (f.)	*soop*	soup
au lait	*oh lai*	bread and milk
sucre (m.)	*s(ee)kr*	sugar
sucré	*s(ee)-kray*	sweetened
tanche (f.)	*taNsh*	tench

tarte (f.)	*tahrt*	(open) tart; flan
tartine (f.)	*tahr-teen*	slice of bread & butter
tête (f.)	*tait*	head
timbale (f.)	*tiN-bahl*	pie-dish
tomate (f.)	*to-maht*	tomato
topinambour (m.)	*to-pee-naN-boor*	Jerusalem artichoke
tortue (f.)	*tor-t(ee)*	turtle
tripe (f.)	*treep*	tripe
tripes à la mode de Caen	*ah lah mod de kaN*	braised tripe and onions
truffe (f.)	*tr(ee)f*	truffle
truite (f.)	*tr(w)eet*	trout
saumonnée	*soh-moh-nay*	salmon trout
tourte (f.)	*toort*	raised pie
tranche (f.)	*traNsh*	slice
napolitaine (See glace)		
turbot (m.)	*t(ee)r-boh*	turbot
vanille (f.)	*vah-neey*	vanilla
veau (m.)	*voh*	veal
ris de veau	*ree de voh*	sweetbread
veau en casserole	*aN kas-rol*	braised veal

vermicelle (m.)	*vair-mee-sail*	vermicelli
viande (f.)	*vyaNd*	meat
viandes froides	*frwahd*	cold buffet
vinaigre (m.)	*vee-naigr*	vinegar
vol-au-vent (m.)	*vo-loh-vaN*	raised pie filled with goose liver, kidney, truffles, etc.
volaille (f.)	*vo-lahy*	poultry; fowl

Part II
Additional Vocabulary
ASKING THE WAY

ASKING ONE'S WAY	POUR DEMANDER SON CHEMIN	poor d'maN-day soN sh'maiN
Which is the way to ...?	Comment va-t-on à ...?	ko-maN vah-ton-ah
The best way to ...?	Le meilleur chemin pour aller à ...?	le mai-y(ai)r sh'maiN poo-rah-lay ah
Where does this road go to?	Où mène cette route?	oo main sait root
In what direction is ...?	Quelle est la direction pour ...?	kai-lai la dee-raik-syoN poor

Is this the way to . . . ?	Est-ce bien le chemin pour . . . ?	*ais'byaiN le sh'maiN poor*
Excuse me, sir, where is the bus stop?	Pardon, monsieur, où est l'arrêt de l'autobus?	*pahr-doN miss-y(ay) oo ai lah-rai de loh-toh-b(ee)s*
Where can I find a bus for . . . ?	Où trouverai-je un autobus pour . . . ?	*oo troov'rai zhe (ai)N noh-toh-b(ee)s poor*
Does this bus go to . . . ?	Cet autobus va-t-il à . . . ?	*sai-toh-toh-b(ee)s vah-tee-lah*
In what direction must I go?	De quel côté me faut-il aller?	*de kail koh-tay me foh-tee-lah-lay*
Do you pass . . . ?	Est-ce que vous passez par . . . ?	*aisk'voo pah-say par*
Where do I have to get off?	Où me faut-il descendre?	*oo me foh-teel dais-saNdr*
Do I get out here?	Dois-je descendre ici?	*dwahzhe dais-saNdr ee see*
Would you be good enough to direct me to . . . ?	Pourriez-vous m'indiquer le chemin de . . . ?	*poor-yay voo miN-dee-kay le sh'maiN de*
Is it far from here to?	Est-ce loin d'ici à . . . ?	*ais lwaiN dee-see ah*

Can I walk there?	Est-ce que je peux y aller à pied?	aisk'zhe p(ay)-zee ah-lay ah pyay
It is about twenty minutes' walk	C'est à environ vingt minutes de marche	sai-tah aN-vee-roN vaiN mee-n(ee)t de mahrsh
Go straight on	Allez tout droit	ah-lay too drwah
Take the first on the right (left)	Prenez la première à droite (gauche)	pre-nay lah prem-yai-rah drwaht (gohsh)
Cross the road (square)	Traversez la rue (place)	trah-vair-say lah r(ee) (plahs)
near here	près d'ici	prai dee-see
far from here	loin d'ici	lwaiN dee see
on the right	à droite	ah drwaht
on the left	à gauche	ah gohsh
at the corner of the street	au coin de la rue	oh kwaiN de la r(ee)
underground (subway)	le métro	may-troh
taxi	le taxi	tah-xee
to get in	monter	moN-tay
to get out	descendre	dais-saNdr
main road	la grand'route	graN-root

side road	un chemin de traverse	*sh'maiN de trah vairs*
crossroads	le carrefour	*kahr-foor*
a fork (in the road)	une bifurcation	*bee-f(ee)r-kas-yoN*
a turning	un tournant	*toor-naN*

TRAVELLING

TRAVELLING	LES VOYAGES (m.pl.)	*vwah-yahzh*
the journey	le voyage	*vwah-yahzh*
to travel, to make a journey	voyager	*vwah-yah-zhay*
to go abroad	aller à l'étranger	*ah-lay ah-lay-traN-zhay*
to the seaside	au bord de la mer	*oh bor de lah mair*
into the country	à la campagne	*ah lah kaN-pahny*
to the mountains	à la montagne	*ah lah moN-tahny*
by train	en chemin de fer	*aN sh'miN de fair*
by boat	en bateau	*aN bah-toh*

by car	en auto	*aN-oh-toh*
by air	en avion	*aN-ahv-yoN*
on foot	à pied	*ah pyay*
on a bicycle	à bicyclette	*ah bee-see-klait*
by land	par terre	*pahr tair*
by sea	par mer	*pahr mair*
by hovercraft	par l'aéroglisseur	*pahr lah-ay-ro-glees-(ai)r*
business journey	le voyage d'affaires	*le vwah-yahzh dah-fair*
pleasure (holiday) trip	le voyage d'agrément	*le vwah-yahzh dahg-ray-maN*
to travel by motorail	voyager par le TAC	*Vwah-ya-zhay pahr le tay-ah-say*
by helicopter	en hélicoptère	*aN ai-lee-cop-tair*
journey for a change of air (for health reasons)	le voyage pour rétablir la santé	*le vwah-yahzh poor ray-tahb-leerla saN-tay*
journey there	aller (m.)	*al-lay*
journey back	retour (m.)	*re-toor*
break in journey	une interruption	*aiN-tai-r(ee)ps-yoN*
round trip (circular tour)	le voyage circulaire	*le vwah-yahzh seerk(ee)-lair*

a long journey	un grand voyage	*(ai)N graN vwah-yahzh*
trip round the world	le voyage autour du monde	*vwah-yahzh oh-toor d(ee) moNd*
route	l'itinéraire (m.)	*ee-tee-nay-rair*
passport (with visa)	le passeport (visé)	*pahs-por (vee-zay)*
tourist agency	une agence de voyage	*ah-zhaNs de vwah-yahzh*
time-table	un horaire	*oh-rair*
railway time-table	un indicateur des chemins de fer	*iN-dee-kah-t(ai)r day sh'miN de fair*
time of departure	heure (f.) du départ	*(ai)r d(ee) day-pahr*
time of arrival	heure d'arrivée	*(ai)r dah-ree-vay*
When is the next train (boat, plane) to ...?	A quelle heure part le prochain train (bateau, avion) pour...?	*ah kai-l (ai)r pahr le proh-shiN triN (bah-toh, ahv-yoN) poor*
When does it arrive at ...?	Quand arrive-t-on à ...?	*kaN-tah-reev-toN ah*
booking office	le guichet	*gee-shai*
ticket	le billet	*bee-yai*
return ticket	billet d'aller et retour	*bee-yai dah-lay ay re-toor*

single ticket	billet simple	bee-yai siNpl
sleeping-car ticket	billet de wagon-lit	bee-yai de vah-goN-lee
reduced price	prix-réduit	pree ray-d(w)ee
supplement	billet supplémentaire	bee-yai s(ee)p-lay-maN-tair
platform-ticket	billet de quai	bee-yai de kay
season ticket	carte d'abonnement	kart dah-bon-maN
available (good) for	valable pour . . .	vah-lahbl poor
How long does my ticket run?	Combien de temps mon billet est-il valable?	koN-byain de taN moN bee-yai ai-teel vah-lahbl
to book a seat	retenir une place	re-te-neer (ee)n plahs
corner (window) seat	un coin de fenêtre	kwaiN de f'naitr
facing the engine	face à la machine	fahs ah lah mah-sheen
with back to the engine	face à l'arrière	fahs ah lahr-yair
two seats side by side	deux places à côté	d(ay) plahs ah koh-tay
two seats opposite each other	deux places en vis-à-vis	d(ay) plah-saN vee-zah-vee
a berth in the sleeping car	une couchette dans un wagon-lit	(ee)n koo-shait daN-z(ai)N vah-goN lee

an upper (lower) berth	une couchette supérieure (inférieure)	(ee)n koo-shait s(ee)pair-y(air) (aiN-fayr-y(air)
a sleeping compartment	un wagon-lit	(ai)N vah-goN lee
THE LUGGAGE	**LES BAGAGES**	bah-gahzh
heavy luggage	les gros bagages	groh bah-gahzh
light luggage	les petits bagages	p'tee bah-gahzh
trunk	la malle	mahl
suit-case	la valise	vah-leez
travelling-bag	le sac de voyage	sakh de vwah-yahzh
case, chest	la caisse	kais
rucksack	le sac à dos	sahk ah doh
cushion (air-)	le coussin (à air)	koo-siN ah air
basket	le panier	pahn-yay
hamper	le panier à provisions	pahn-yay ah prohveez-yoN
travelling-rug	la couverture de voyage	koo-vair-t(ee)r de vwah-yahzh
to do one's packing	faire ses malles	fair say mahl
to pack something	emballer quelque chose	aN-bah-lay kailk shohz

to unpack	déballer	day-bah-lay
to send in advance by passenger train	expédier par la grande vitesse	aiks-payd-yay pahr lah graNd vee-tais
by goods train	par la petite vitesse	pahr lah p'teet vee-tais
luggage office	enregistrement des bagages	aN-re-geest-re-maN day bah-gahzh
luggage ticket	le bulletin de bagages	b(ee)l-tiN de bah-gahzh
porter	le porteur	por-t(ai)r
fetch from the cloak-room	aller prendre à la con-signe	ah-lay praNdr ah lah koN-seeny
take our luggage to the train (boat)	porter nos bagages au train (bateau)	por-tay noh bah-gahzh oh traiN (bah-toh)
to weigh	peser	pe-zay
overweight	excédent	ek-say-daN
to insure	assurer	ah-s(ee)-ray
to leave in the cloak-room	laisser en consigne	lai-say aN koN-seeny
three pieces (of lug-gage)	trois colis	trwah koh-lee

CUSTOMS	LA DOUANE	doo-ahn
to examine the luggage	visiter les bagages	vee-zee-tay lay bah-gazh
custom-house	la douane	doo-ahn
custom-house officer	le douanier	doo-ahn-yay
duty free	exempt de droits	aig-zaN de drwah
liable to duty	soumis aux droits	soo-mee oh drwah
to pay duty	payer les droits	pay-yay lay drwah
smuggling	la contrebande	koNtr-baNd
Have you anything to declare?	Avez-vous quelque chose à déclarer?	ah-vay voo kailk shohz ah day-klah-ray
Duty-free allowance	Marchandises hors-taxe	mar-shaN-dees or-tax
I have nothing to declare	Je n'ai rien à déclarer	zhe nay ryaiN ah day-klah-ray
for personal use	des effets à mon usage	day-zai-fay ah mon(ee)-zahzh
Is there any duty to pay on this?	Cela paie-t-il des droits?	s'lah pay-teel day drwah
Have you any cigars?	Avez-vous des cigares?	ah-vay voo day see-gahr

I haven't any	Je n'en ai pas	*zhe naN-nai pah*
I have only five	J'en ai seulement cinq	*zhaN-nai s(ai) l'-maN saiNk*
How many cigars are free?	Combien de cigares peut-on passer en franchise?	*coN-byaiN de see-gahr p(ay)-toN pah-say aN fraN-sheez*
How much have I to pay?	Combien ai-je à payer?	*koN-byaiN aizh' ah pay-yay*
What is in there?	Qu'avez-vous là-de-dans?	*kah-vay voo lah d'daN*
Only toilet things	Seulement des affaires de toilette	*s(ai)l-maN day-zah-fair de twah-lait*
These clothes have already been worn	Ces effets ont déjà été portés	*say-zay-fai oN day-zhah ay-tay por-tay*
Be careful please, these are breakable things	Faites attention s.v.p., ici il y a des choses fragiles	*fait-zah-taNs-yoN seel voo plai, ee-see eel-yah day shohz frah-zheel*
You can shut your trunks	Vous pouvez refermer vos malles	*voo poo-vay re-fer-may voh mahl*

RAILWAY	LE CHEMIN DE FER	*le sh'miN d'fair*
(See also Travelling, Luggage, Customs, Journey)		
by rail	**par le train**	*pahr le traiN*
the train starts	**le train part**	*le traiN pahr*
stops	**s'arrête**	*sah-rait*
goes through	**ne s'arrête pas**	*ne .sah-rait-pah*
arrives	**arrive**	*ah-reev*
fast train	**rapide**	*rah-peed*
express	**express**	*aiks-prais*
slow train	**omnibus**	*om-nee-b(ee)s*
through train	**direct**	*dee-rekt*
passenger train	**de voyageurs**	*de vwah-yah-zh(ai)r*
goods train	**de marchan-dises**	*de mahr-shaN-deez*
to catch (to miss) the train	**arriver pour (man-quer) le train**	*ah-ree-vay poor (maN-kay) le traiN*

to get in	monter dans le train	*moN-tay daN le traiN*
to get out	descendre du train	*dais-saN dr d(ee) traiN*
the train has no connection	le train n'a pas de correspondance	*le traiN nah pah de ko-rais-poN-daNs*
trains to . . .	les trains à destination de . . .	*lay traiN ah dais-tee-nahs-yoN de*
trains from . . .	les trains venant de . . .	*lay traiN ve-naN de*
station	la gare	*gahr*
booking-office	le guichet	*gee-shay*
platform-ticket	le billet de quai	*bee-yai de kay*
automatic machine	le distributeur	*dees-tree-b(ee)-t(ai)r*
waiting room	la salle d'attente	*sahl dah-taNt*
refreshment room	le buffet	*b(ee)-fai*
this way to the trains for . . .	direction de . . .	*dee-raiks-yoN de*
platform	le quai	*kai*
engine	la locomotive	*loh-koh-moh-teev*
carriage	le wagon	*vah-goN*
	la voiture	*vwah-t(ee)r*
carriage door	la portière	*port-yair*
sleeping-car	le wagon-lit	*vah-goN-lee*
dining-car	le wagon-restaurant	*vah-goN res-toh-raN*

station-master	le chef de gare	*shaif de gahr*
guard	le contrôleur	*koN-troh l(ai)r*
compartment	le compartiment	*koN-pahr-tee-maN*
'smokers'	'fumeurs'	*f(ee)-m(ai)r*
seat	une place	*plahs*
corner seat (next to the window)	un coin de fenêtre	*kwaiN de f'naitr*
corridor	le couloir	*koo-lwahr*
to put on the rack	mettre dans le filet	*maitr daN le fee-lay*
to open the window	baisser la glace	*bai-say lah glahs*
to raise (close) the window	remonter la glace	*re-moN-tay lah glahs*
to turn on the heating	ouvrir la chaleur	*oov-reer lah sha-l(ai)r*
to turn off the heating	fermer la chaleur	*fair-may lah sha-l(ai)r*
Is this the train for ...?	Est-ce là le train pour ...?	*ai se lah le traiN poor*
Has the train for ... arrived?	Le train pour ... est-il déjà là?	*le traiN poor ... ai-teel day-zhah lah*
The train is ... minutes late	Le train a un retard de ... minutes	*le traiN ah (ai)N re-tahr de ... meen(ee)t*

Is there a through carriage to . . . in the train?	Y a-t-il dans le train un wagon direct pour . . .?	yah-teel daN le traiN (ai)N vah-goN dee-raikt poor
From which platform does the train for . . . start	De quel quai part le train pour . . .?	de kel kay par le traiN poor
Is this seat taken?	Cette place est-elle retenue?	sait plahs ai-tail re-te-n(ee)
Is there any room here?	Y a-t-il encore une place?	yah-teel aN-ko-r (ee)n plahs
There is no seat left	Il n'y a plus de place	eel nyah pl(ee) de plahs
Take your seats!	En voiture s.v.p.	aN vwah-t(ee)r seel voo plai
Do you mind if I smoke (open the window, shut the door)?	Est-ce que vous permettez que je fume (baisse la glace, ferme la portière)?	aisk'voo pair-mai-tay k'zhe f(ee)m (bais lah glahs, fairm lah port-yair)
How long does the train stop here?	Combien de temps le train s'arrête-t-il ici?	koN-byaiN de taN le traiN sah-rai-teel ee-see

What time do we arrive?	Quand arriverons-nous?	kaN-tah-reev'roN noo
SHIPS	**LES NAVIRES** (m.pl.)	*nah-veer*
(See also At the seaside, page 143)		
liner	le paquebot	*pahk-boh*
cruise liner	le navire croisière	*le nah-veer crwahz-ee-air*
car ferry	le ferry	*le fe-ree*
drive-on-ferry	le ferry drive-on	*le fe-ree drive-on*
steamer	le vapeur	*vah-p(ai)r*
cargo boat	le cargo	*kahr-goh*
sailing boat	le bateau à voiles	*bah-tohah vwahl*
fishing boat	de pêche	*de paish*
motor-boat	à moteur	*ah moh-t(ai)r*
rowing boat	à rames	*ah rahm*
yacht	le yacht	*ee-aht*
lifeboat	le canot de sauvetage	*kah-noh de sohv-tahzh*
lifebelt	la ceinture de sauvetage	*saiN-t(ee)r de sohv-tahzh*

port	le port	por
lighthouse	le phare	fahr
to embark	s'embarquer	saN-bahr-kay
out at sea	au large	oh lahrzh
to land	débarquer	day-bahr-kay
crossing	la traversée	trah-vair-say
calm sea	la mer calme	mair kahlm
choppy sea	agitée	ah-zhee-tay
rough sea	mauvaise	moh-vaiz
high sea	grosse	gros
deck	le pont	poN
upper deck	le pont supérieur	poN s(ee)-payr-y(ai)r
boat deck	le pont d'embarcation	poN daN-bahr-kahs-yoN
promenade deck	le pont promenade	poN prom-nahd
prow (bow)	la proue	proo
stern	la poupe	poop
cabin	la cabine	kah-been
berth	la couchette	koo-shait
steward	le garçon (de cabine)	gahr-soN de kah-been
	le steward	ste-wahr

stewardess	la femme de chambre;	fahm de shaN-br
	la stewardess	ste-wahr-dais
purser	le commissaire	ko-mee-sair
captain	le capitaine	kah-pee-tain
sea sickness	le mal de mer	mahl de mair
basin	la cuvette	k(ee)-vait

FLYING   **L'AVIATION**   *ahv-yahs-yoN*

to fly	voler	vo-lay
aeroplane	un avion	ahv-yon
airliner	l'avion de ligne	lahv-yon de leen-ye
jumbo-jet	l'appareil jumbo-jet	lahp-ahray jumbo-jet
supersonic airliner	un avion supersonique	(ai)N ahv-yon s(ee)p-air-son-eek
by air	par avion	pah-rahv-yon
aerodrome	un aérodrome	(ai)N ay-roh-drom
departure gate	la porte de départ	la port de day-parh
duty-free lounge	le salon d'attente hors-taxe	le sah-loN daht aNt or-tax
duty-free shop	la boutique hors-taxe	boo-teek or-tax
boarding ticket	la carte d'embarque-ment	cahrt deN-bark-maN

in-flight meal	le repas en vol	repahs-aN vol
baggage allowance	les bagages autorisés en franchise	bah-gazh oh-tor-eezai aN fraN-sheez
charter flight	le vol charter	vol charter
ground hostess	l'hôtesse au sol	loht-ess oh sol
air hostess	l'hôtesse de l'air	loht-ess de lair
arrival gate	la porte d'arrivée	port dahr-eevay
luggage collection area	l'aire de réception des bagages	lair de ray-sep-sioN day bahg-ahzh
air terminal	l'aérogare	lai-roh-gahr
airport bus	le car de l'aéroport	cahr de lai-roh-port
delay due to engine trouble fog	le retard dû à une panne de moteur au brouillard	re-tahr d(ee) ah (ee)n pahn de moht(ay)r oh broo-yahr
cotton wool	ouate (f.)	waht
air sickness	le mal de l'air	mahl de lair
paper bags (for air sickness)	des cornets (pour le mal de l'air)	kor-nai
to take off	décoller	day-ko-lay
to rise	monter	moN-tay
to fly over	survoler	ś(ee)r-vo-lay

to land	atterrir	*ah-tai-reer*
speed	la vitesse	*vee-tais*
height	l'altitude	*ahl-tee-t(ee)d*

MOTOR-CAR   L'AUTOMOBILE   *oh-toh-moh-beel*

(See also Asking one's
way)

Note: In speaking of the make of a car, one says: "Une Citroen" –
"Une Austin," etc. Likewise when referring to one's car, one says: "Ma
Voiture."

a 6-cylinder car	une six-cylindres	*see see-liNdr*
a saloon car	une conduite intérieure	*koN-d(w)eet aiN-tay-ry(ai)r*
sports car	la voiture sport	*lah vwah-t(ee)r spor*
V8 engine	le moteur huit cylindres en V	*moh-t(ai)r wee cee-liNdr aN vay*
estate car	la commerciale	*com-airs-yahl*
automatic trans-mission car	la voiture avec boîte automatique	*vwah-t(ee)r ah-vek bwaht oh-toh-mah teek*

a motor-bicycle	une motocyclette	*moh-toh-seek-lait*
driving licence	le permis de conduire	*pair-mee de koN-d(w)eer*
to start up (the engine)	mettre (le moteur) en marche	*maitr le moh-t(ai)r aN mahrsh*
to engage the first (second, third) gear	mettre en première (deuxième, troisième) vitesse	*maitr aN prem-yair d(ay)z-yaim, trwahz-yaim) vee-tais*
to engage the reverse gear	mettre en marche arrière	*maitr-aN mahrsh ahr-yair*
with the throttle full open; flat out	à plein gaz	*ah plaiN gahz*
international driving permit	le permis de conduire international	*pair-mee de coN-dweer iN-tair-nah-syon-ahl*
to hoot	klaxonner	*klahk-soh-n(ay)*
to overtake	doubler	*doob-lay*
to apply the brakes	freiner	*frai-nay*
to accelerate	accélérer	*ak-say-lay-ray*
to slow down	ralentir	*rah-laN-teer*
to park	stationner	*stahs-yo-nay*
double-de-clutch	le double débrayage	*doobl day-brah-yahzh*

| to 'rev' | accélérer sur place | *ahk-say-lay-ray s(ee)r plahs* |

PETROL STATION — LE DÉPOT D'ESSENCE — *day-poh dai-saNs*

to fill up with petrol	faire le plein d'essence	*fair le plaiN dai-saNs*
oil	d'huile	*d(w)eel*
water	d'eau	*doh*
to change the oil	changer l'huile	*shaN-zhay l(w)eel*
to grease the car	graisser la voiture	*grai-say lah vwaht(ee)r*
to wash the car	laver la voiture	*lah-vay lah vwaht(ee)r*
to inflate the tyres	gonfler les pneus	*goN-flay lay pn(ay)*
a spare tin	un bidon de secours	*bee-doN de s'koor*
to top up the battery (with distilled water)	remettre de l'eau distillée dans les accus	*re-maitr de loh deesteel-ay daN layz ak(ee)*
the windscreen washers	les essuie-glaces	*lay aiswee glahs*
self-service petrol station	station libre-service	*stah-syon leebr sair-vees*

REPAIR SHOP	UN ATELIER DE RÉPARATION	*ah-tel-yay de ray-pah-rahs-yoN*
a breakdown	une panne	*pahn*
out of order	ne fonctionne pas	*ne foNks-yon pah*
broken	cassé	*kah-say*
broken fan belt	la courroie de ventilateur cassée	*coo-rwah de vaN-teel-ah-t(ai)r kah-say*
burnt	brûlé	*br(ee)-lay*
choked	bouché	*boo-shay*
overheated	chauffé	*shoh-fay*
bent	faussé	*foh-say*
worn-out	usé	*(ee)-zay*
squeaks	grince	*griNs*
to repair	réparer	*ray-pah-ray*
to clear (a pipe), etc.	déboucher	*day-boo-shay*
to change	changer	*shaN-zhay*
to charge	charger	*shar-zhay*
to adjust	ajuster	*ah-zh(ee)s-tay*
to clean	nettoyer	*nai-twah-yay*
to tow in	remorquer	*re-mor-kay*

a repairer	un dépanneur, un réparateur	day-pah-n(ai)r, ray-pah-rah-t(ai)r
BODYWORK	**LA CARROSSERIE**	*kah-ros'ree*
hood	la capote	*kah-pot*
windscreen	le pare-brise	*pahr-breez*
windscreen wiper	l'essuie glace	*aiswee glahs*
exhaust pipe	le tuyau d'échappement	*t(ee)-yo day-shahp-maN*
sidelights	les feux de position	*f(ay) de poh-zees-yon*
door	la portière	*port-yair*
seat	le siège	*syaizh*
window	la glace	*glahs*
headlight	le phare	*fahr*
hooter	le klaxon	*clah-ksoN*
CHASSIS	**LE CHASSIS**	*shah-see*
back axle	le pont arrière	*poN ahr-yair*
front axle	l'essieu avant	*les-y(ay) ah-vaN*
steering gear	la direction	*dee-reks-yoN*

steering wheel	le volant	*vo-laN*
springs	les ressorts	*rai-sor*
bonnet	le capot	*ka-poh*
brakes	les freins (m.pl.)	*fraiN*
petrol tank	le réservoir d'essence	*ray-zair-vwahr dai-saNs*
wheel	la roue	*roo*
spare wheel	la roue de rechange	*roo de re-shaNzh*
tyre	le pneu	*pn(ay)*

ENGINE — LE MOTEUR — *moht(ai)r*

carburettor	le carburateur	*kahr-b(ee)rah-t(ai)r*
clutch	l'embrayage	*aN-brai-yahzh*
crankshaft	le vilebrequin	*veel-bre-kaiN*
ignition	l'allumage	*ah-l(ee)-mahzh*
magneto	la magnéto	*mahn-yay-toh*
battery	la batterie	*baht'ree*
self starter	le démarreur	*day-mah-r(ai)r*
starting handle	la manivelle	*mah-nee-vail*
sparking plug	la bougie	*boo-zhe*
valve	la soupape	*soo-pahp*

| automatic transmission | **la boîte automatique** | *bwaht oh-toh-mah-teek* |
| hydrolastic suspension | **la suspension hydrolastique** | *la s(ee)s-peN-syon eed-roh-lahst-eek* |

THE HOTEL

| AT THE HOTEL | A L'HOTEL | *ah loh-tail* |

| Which hotel could you recommend? | **Quel hôtel pouvez-vous me recommander?** | *ke-loh-tail poo-vay voo me re-ko-maN-day* |
| Have you any rooms vacant? | **Avez-vous des chambres libres?** | *ah-vay voo day shaNbr leebr* |

What is the price per day (week, month)?	Combien est-ce par jour (semaine, mois)?	koN-byiN ais' pahr zhoor (s'main, mwah)
a single room	une chambre pour une personne	(ee)n shaNbr poor (ee)n pair-son
a double room	une chambre à deux lits	(ee)n shaNbr d(ay) lee
a room with a private bath	une chambre avec salle de bain	(ee)n shaNbrah-vek sahl de'baiN
bedroom and sitting room	une chambre avec salon	(ee)n shaNbrah-vek sah-loN
I will take this room (these rooms)	Je prendrai cette chambre (ces chambres)	zhe praN-dray sait shaNbr (say shaNbr)
Have my luggage sent up, please	Faites monter mes bagages, s'il vous plaît	fait moN-tay may bah-gahzh seel voo plai
I should like to have a bath	Je voudrais prendre un bain	zhe vood-rai praNd-r (ai)N baiN
hall	le vestibule	ves-tee-b(ee)l
dining-room	la salle à manger	sah-lah-maN-zhay
bathroom	la salle de bain	sahl de baiN

lavatory	les cabinets	*kah-bee-nay*
lift	un ascenseur	*ahs-saN-s(ai)r*
bell	la sonnette	*so-nait*
key	la clef	*klay*
manager	le gérant	*zhay-raN*
porter	le portier	*por-tyay*
boots	le valet	*vah-lay*
chambermaid	la femme de chambre	*fahm de'shaNbr*
page boy	le chasseur	*shah-s(ai)r*
lift-boy	le liftier	*lift-yay*
the bill (for a meal)	l'addition	*ah-dees-yoN*
the (hotel) bill	la note	*not*
tip	le pourboire	*poor-bwahr*

TOWN AND COUNTRY

TOWN AND COUNTRY	LA VILLE ET LA CAMPAGNE	*lah veel ay lah kaN-pany*
In Town:	En Ville:	*aN veel:*
a manufacturing town	une ville industrielle	*veel aiN-d(ee)s-tree-ail*
a commercial town	commerciale	*ko-mairs-yahl*
a provincial town	provinciale	*proh-viNs-yahl*
capital	la capitale	*kah-pee-tahl*
the inhabitants	les habitants	*ah-bee-taN*
the centre of the town	le centre de la ville	*saNtr de lah veel*
quarter; part of the town	le quartier[1]	*kahrt-yay*

[1] In Paris: **arrondissement** *ah-roN-dees-maN*

suburbs	les faubourgs (m.pl.)	*fohb-oor*
surroundings	les environs (m.pl.)	*aN-vee-roN*
main street	rue principale	*r(ee) priN-see-pahl*
side street	latérale	*lah-tay-rahl*

pavement (side-walk)	le trottoir	*trot-wahr*
roadway	la chaussée	*shoh-say*
to cross the street	traverser la rue	*trah-vair-say lah r(ee)*
crossing	le carrefour	*kahr-foor*
at the corner	au coin	*oh kwaiN*
square	la place	*plahs*
square with garden	le square	*skwahr*
market	le marché	*mahr-shay*
botanical gardens	le jardin botanique	*zhahr-daiN boh-tah-neek*
zoological gardens	le jardin zoologique	*zhahr-daiN zo-oloh-zheek*
bridge	le pont	*poN*
river	le fleuve	*fl(ai)v*
chapel	la chapelle	*shah-pail*
church	une église	*ay-gleez*
cathedral	la cathédrale	*kah-tay-drahl*
factory	l'usine	*ee-zeen*
museum	le musée	*m(ee)-zay*
exhibition	une exposition	*eks-poh-zee-syoN*
school	une école	*ay-kol*

town-hall	la mairie	*mai-ree*
library	la bibliothèque	*bee-blee-oh-taik*
castle	un château	*shah-toh*
policeman	un agent	*ah-zhaN*
police-station	le poste de police	*post de po-lees*
fire-brigade	les pompiers	*poN-pyay*
bank	la banque	*baNk*
hotel	un hôtel	*oh-tail*
cinema	le cinéma	*see-nay-mah*
theatre	le théâtre	*tay-ahtr*
embassy	une ambassade	*aN-bah-sahd*
tower	la tour	*toor*
statue	le monument	*mo-n(ee)-maN*
to go sight-seeing	visiter les curiosités	*vee-zee-tay lay k(ee)r-yoh-zee-tay*
traffic	la circulation	*seer-k(ee)lahs-yoN*

| IN THE COUNTRY | A LA CAMPAGNE | *ah lah kaN-pany* |

village	le village	*vee-lahzh*
hamlet	le hameau	*ah-moh*
farm	une ferme	*fairm*

mill	le moulin	*moo-liN*
forest	la forêt	*fo-ray*
wood	le bois	*bwah*
field	le champ	*shaN*
stream	la rivière	*reev-yair*
brook	le ruisseau	*r(w)ee-soh*
tree	un arbre	*ahrbr*
flower	la fleur	*fl(ai)r*
hill	la colline	*ko-leen*
mountain	la montagne	*moN-tahny*
valley	la vallée	*vah-lay*
cottage	la chaumière	*shohm-yair*
castle	le château	*shah-toh*
barn	une grange	*graNzh*
orchard	le verger	*vair-zhay*
kitchen garden	le jardin potager	*zhahr-daiN poh-tah-zhay*
flower garden	le jardin d'agrément	*zhahr-daiN dah-gray-maN*
well	le puits	*p(w)ee*
hedge	la haie	*ai*
road	la route; le chemin	*root; sh'miN*

highway	la grande route	*graN-root*
footpath	le sentier	*saN-tyay*
pond	un étang	*ay-taN*
lake	le lac	*lahk*
bird	un oiseau	*wah-zoh*
fly	une mouche	*moosh*
butterfly	le papillon	*pah-pee-yoN*
ant	la fourmi	*foor-mee*
gnat	le moustique	*moos-teek*
bee	une abeille	*ah-baiy*
wasp	la guêpe	*gaip*

| AT THE SEASIDE (See also Ships) | AU BORD DE LA MER | *oh bor de lah mair* |

beach	la plage	*plahzh*
coast	la côte	*koht*
sea-bathe	un bain de mer	*baiN de mair*
to bathe	se baigner	*bain-yay*
bathing cap	le bonnet de bain	*bo-nai de baiN*
shoes	les sandales de bain	*saN-dahl de baiN*
trunks	le slip	*sleep*

wrap	**le peignoir de bain**	*pain-ywahr de baiN*
hut	**la cabine de bain**	*kah-been de baiN*
pier	**la jetée**	*zhe-tay*
sand	**le sable**	*sahbl*
breakwater	**le brise-lames**	*breez-lahm*
swimming	**la nage**	*nahzh*
to swim	**nager**	*nah-zhay*
to swim across	**traverser à la nage**	*tra-vair-say ah lah nazh*
high tide	**la marée haute**	*mah-ray oht*
low tide	**la marée basse**	*mah-ray bahs*
reef	**un écueil**	*ay-k(ai)y*
shingle	**les galets** (m.pl.)	*gah-lay*
to go fishing	**aller à la pêche**	*ah-lay ah lah paish*

THE POST OFFICE	**LE BUREAU DE POSTE**	*le b(ee)-roh de post*
Where is the nearest post office?	**Où est le bureau de poste le plus proche?**	*oo ai le b(ee)-roh de post le pl(ee) prosh*

I want some stamps	Je désire des timbres	*zhe day-zeer day taiN-br*
What is the postage to . . .?	Quel est l'affranchissement pour . . .?	*kai-lai lah-fraN-shees-maN poor*
to hand in a telegram	remettre un télégramme	*re-maitr (ai)N tay-lay-grahm*
What is the charge per word?	Quel est le tarif par mot?	*kai-lai le tah-reef pahr moh*
reply prepaid	réponse payée	*ray-poNs pay-yay*
I want to register this letter	Je désire faire recommander cette lettre	*zhe day-zeer fair re-ko-maN-day sait laitr*
Are there any letters for me?	Y a-t-il des lettres pour moi?	*ee ah-teel day laitr poor mwah*
Please forward my letters to this address	Voulez-vous avoir l'obligeance de faire suivre mes lettres à cette adresse	*voo-lay voo-zahv-wahr lob-lee-zhaNs De fair sweevr may laitr ah sait-tahd-rais*
to be called for	poste restante	*post rais-taNt*
air-mail	par avion	*pah-rahv-yoN*
letter-box	une boîte aux lettres	*(ee)n bwah-toh laitr*
money-order	un mandat-poste	*manN-dah post*

parcel	le paquet	*pah-kai*
registered letter	une lettre recommandée	*laitr re-ko-maN-day*
printed matter	un imprimé	*iN-pree-may*
sample	échantillon	*ay-shaN-tee-yoN*
telephone	le téléphone	*tay-lay-fohn*
to telephone	téléphoner	*tay-lay-foh-nay*
telephone number	le numéro d'appel	*n(ee)-may-roh dah-pail*
I wish to 'phone to London	Je voudrais téléphoner à Londres	*zhe vood-rai tay-lay-foh-nay ah loNdr*
to take off the receiver	décrocher le récepteur	*day-kro-shay le ray-saip-t(ai)r;*
to hang up the receiver	accrocher le récepteur	*ah-kro-shay le ray-saip-t(ai)r*
Connect me with number 6743, please	Mettez-moi en communication avec le numéro soixante-sept, quarante-trois, s'il vous plaît	*mai-tay mwah aN kom(ee)-nee-kahs-yoN ah-vek le n(ee)-may-roh swah-saNt-sait kah-raNt trwah seel voo plai*
The line is engaged at present	La ligne est occupée à présent	*lah leeny ai-to-k(ee)-pay ah pray-zanN*

disengaged (free) now	libre maintenant	*leebr maiNt-naN*
Are you there, Mr. B.	Allô! C'est vous Monsieur B.?	*ah-loh sai voo*
This is . . . speaking	C'est . . . qui parle	*sai . . . kee pahrl*
I should like to speak to . . .	Je voudrais parler à . . .	*zhe voo-drai pahr-lay ah*

THE RESTAURANT   LE RESTAURANT   *le rais-toh-raN*

Note.—In most French restaurants a small cover charge is made; it is called 'couvert'

grill room	la rôtisserie	*lah ro-tees'ree*
waiter	le garçon	*le gahr-soN*
a table for two	une table pour deux	*(ee)n tahbl poor d(ay)*
the menu	le menu; la carte	*le me-n(ee); lah kahrt*
the wine-list	la carte des vins	*lah kahrt day vaiN*
table d'hôte	à prix fixe	*ah pree feex*
special dishes	les plats du jour	*lay plah d(ee) zhoor*
What will you have (next)?	Que prenez-vous (ensuite)?	*ke pre-nay voo (aN-sweet)*

Can you recommend this?	Pouvez-vous recommander ceci?	*poo-vay voo re-ko-maN-day se-see*
A knife (fork, spoon) is missing	Il me manque un couteau (une fourchette, une cuiller)	*eel me maNk (ai)N-kootoh; (ee)n foor-shait; (ee)n kwee-yair*
Take this away	Emportez ceci	*aN-por-tay se-see*
This is not fresh (clean)	Ceci n'est pas frais (propre)	*se-see nai pah frai (propr)*
Waiter, the bill please	Garçon, l'addition, s'il vous plaît	*gahr-soN lah-dees-yoN seel-voo plai*
You can keep the change	Gardez la monnaie	*gahr-day lah mo-nai*

FOOD

LA NOURRITURE

noo-ree-t(ee)r

fork	une fourchette	*(ee)n foor-shait*
knife	un couteau	*(ai)N koo-toh*
spoon	une cuiller	*(ee)n kwee-yair*
plate	une assiette	*(ee)n ahs-yait*
cruet oil and vinegar	l'huilier (m.)	*(w)eel-yay*
dish	un plat	*(ai)N plah*

napkin	la serviette	*sair-vyait*
a portion	une portion	*pors-yoN*
breakfast	le petit déjeuner	*le p'tee day-zh(ai)-nay*

Note.—The normal French breakfast, un café complet, consists of a roll, butter, coffee or chocolate. It can be obtained in any café. Un café simple, coffee alone.

lunch	le déjeuner	*le day-zh(ai)-nay*
to have lunch	déjeuner	*day-zh(ai)-nay*
dinner	le dîner	*le dee-nay*
to dine	dîner	*dee-nay*
supper	le souper	*le soo-pay*
to have supper	souper	*soo-pay*
meal	le repas	*le re-pah*

almonds	les amandes (f.pl.)	*ah-maNd*
anchovy	l'anchois (m.)	*aN-shwah*
apple	la pomme	*pom*
apricot	l'abricot (m.)	*ah-bree-koh*
artichoke	l'artichaut (m.)	*ahr-tee-shoh*
asparagus	les asperges (f.pl.)	*ahs-pairzh*
bacon	le lard	*lahr*

banana	la banane	*bah-nahn*
bean	le haricot	*ah-ree-koh*
broad beans	les fèves	*faiv*
French beans	les haricots verts	*ah-ree-koh vair*
beef	le bœuf	*b(ai)f*
beef broth	le pot au feu	*po-toh-f(ay)*
beef steak	le bifteck	*beef-taick*
beef tea	le bouillon	*boo-yoN*
beetroot	la betterave	*bait-rahv*
biscuit	le biscuit	*bees kwee*
black currant	le cassis	*kah-see*
bread	le pain	*paiN*
slice of bread	la tartine	*tahr-teen*
breast	la poitrine	*pwah-treen*
broth	le bouillon	*boo-yoN*
Brussels sprouts	les choux de **Bruxelles**	*shoo de br(ee)-sail*
bun	la brioche	*bree-osh*
butter	le beurre	*b(ai)r*
cabbage	le chou	*shoo*
cake	le gâteau	*gah-toh*
carrot	la carotte	*kah-rot*
cauliflower	le chou-fleur	*shoo-fl(ai)r*

celery	le céleri	*sayl'ree*
cheese	le fromage	*fro-mahzh*
cherry	la cerise	*s'reez*
chestnut	le marron	*mah-roN*
chicken	le poulet	*poo-lai*
chocolate	le chocolat	*sho-koh-lah*
chop	la côtelette	*koht-lait*
crab	le crabe	*krahb*
crayfish	la langouste	*laN-goost*
cress	le cresson	*krai-soN*
cucumber	le concombre	*koN-koNbr*
cutlet; chop	la côtelette	*koht-lait*
date	la datte	*dat*
duck	le canard	*kah-nahr*
eel	l'anguille	*aN-geey*
egg	l'œuf:	*(ai)f*
	(pl.: les œufs)	pl.: *(ay)*
boiled egg	œuf à la coque	*(ai)-fah-lah cok*
fried egg	œuf sur le plat	*(ai)f s(ee)r le plah*
hard-boiled egg	œuf dur	*(ai)f d(ee)r*
poached egg	œuf poché	*(ai)f poh-shay*
scrambled egg	œuf brouillé	*(ai)f broo-yay*

fig	la figue	*feeg*
fish	le poisson	*pwah-soN*
fruit	le fruit	*le frwee*
stewed fruit	la compote	*lah koN-pot*
game	le gibier	*zheeb-yay*
grape	le raisin	*rai-zaiN*
goose	une oie	*(ee)n wah*
ham	le jambon	*zhaN-boN*
hare	le lièvre	*lyaivr*
herring	le hareng	*ah-raN*
honey	le miel	*myail*
jam	la confiture	*koN-fee-t(ee)r*
ice-cream	la glace	*glahs*
jelly	la gelée	*zhe-lay*
kidney	le rognon	*ron-yoN*
lamb	l'agneau	*ahn-yoh*
lemon	le citron	*seet-roN*
lentils	les lentilles (f.pl.)	*laN-teey*
lettuce	la laitue	*lai-t(ee)*
liver	le foie	*fwah*
lobster	le homard	*o-mahr*
mackerel	le maquereau	*mahk-roh*

meat	la viande	vyaNd
melon	le melon	me-loN
minced meat	le hachis	ah-shee
milk	le lait	lai
mushroom	le champignon	shaN-peen-yoN
mussel	la moule	mool
mustard	la moutarde	moo-tahrd
mutton	le mouton	moo-toN
leg of mutton	le gigot	zhee-goh
stewed mutton with turnips	le navarin	nah-vah-raiN
nut (walnut)	la noix	nwah
(hazel)	la noisette	nwah-zait
oil	l'huile (f.)	(w)eel
onion	l'oignon	on-yoN
orange	l'orange (f.)	oh-raNzh
oyster	l'huître (f.)	(w)eetr
parsley	le persil	pair-see
paste	la pâte	paht
pastry	la pâtisserie	pah-tees-ree
peach	la pêche	paish
pear	la poire	pwahr

peas	les petits pois (m.pl.)	p'tee pwah
pepper	le poivre	pwahvr
pheasant	le faisan	fai-zaN
pie	le pâté	pah-tay
pineapple	l'ananas (m.)	an-nah-nahs
plum	la prune	pr(ee)n
pork	le porc	por
potato	la pomme de terre	pom de tair
fried potatoes	pommes frites	pom freet
boiled potatoes	pommes nature	pom nah-t(ee)r
mashed potatoes	purée de pommes	p(ee)-ray d'pom
poultry, wing, leg	la volaille, l'aile, la cuisse	volahy, ail, k(w)ees
rabbit	le lapin	lah-paiN
radish	le radis	rah-dee
raspberry	la framboise	fraN-bwahz
red currant	la groseille rouge	gro-zaiy roozh
rice	le riz	ree
roast beef	le rosbif	roz-beef
roast; joint	le rôti	ro-tee
roll	le petit pain	p'tee paiN
crescent-shaped roll	le croissant	krwah-saN

rusks	des biscottes (f.pl.)	*bees-kot*
salade	la salade	*sah-lahd*
salmon	le saumon	*soh-moN*
salt	le sel	*sail*
sausage	la saucisse	*soh-sees*
sausages (dry)	les saucissons (m.pl.)	*soh-see-soN*
semolina	la semoule	*semool*
shrimps	les crevettes (f.pl.)	*kre-vait*
snack	un casse-croûte	*kahs-kroot*
soup	le potage, la soupe	*po-tahzh, soop*
spinach	les épinards	*ay-pee-nahr*
steak	le bifteck	*beef-taick*
stew	le ragoût	*rah-goo*
strawberry	la fraise	*fraiz*
sugar	le sucre	*s(ee)kr*
toast	du pain grillé	*paiN gree-yay*
tomato	la tomate	*to-maht*
tongue	la langue	*laNg*
trout	la truite	*tr(w)eet*
turkey	le dindon	*daiN-doN*
veal	le veau	*voh*
vegetable	le légume	*lay-g(ee)m*

| vinegar | le vinaigre | *vee-naigr* |
| watercress | le cresson | *kre-soN* |

DRINKS | ## LES BOISSONS | *bwah-soN* |

a glass of ...	un verre de ...	(*ai*)*N vair d*e
a cup of ...	une tasse de ...	(*ee*)*n tahs d*e
a bottle of ...	une bouteille de ...	(*ee*)*n boo-taiy d*e
half-bottle	une demi-bouteille	*d'mee boo-taiy*
a champagne glass	une coupe à champagne	(*ee*)*n koo-pah shaN-pahny*
coffee	le café	*kah-fay*
black coffee	café nature	*kah-fay nah-t*(*ee*)*r*
coffee with milk	café au lait	*kah-fay oh lai*
iced coffee	café glacé	*kah-fay glah-say*
tea	le thé	*tay*
milk (cold)	le lait froid	*lai frwah*
milk (hot)	le lait chaud	*lai shoh*
cocoa	le cacao	*kah-kah-oh*
water	l'eau (f.)	*oh*
mineral waters	eaux minérales (f.pl.)	*oh-mee-nay-rahl*
lemonade	la limonade	*lee-moh-nahd*

lemon squash	**citron pressé**	*seet-roN prai-say*
iced lemonade	**citronnade glacée**	*seet-ro-nahd glah-say*
orange squash	**orange pressée**	*oh-raNzh prai-say*
iced orangeade	**orangeade glacée**	*oh-raN-zhahd glah-say*
wine	**du vin**	*d(ee) vaiN*
white bordeaux wine	**bordeaux blanc**	*bor-doh-blaN*
red bordeaux wine (claret)	**bordeaux rouge**	*bor-doh roozh*
mulled wine	**vin chaud**	*vaiN shoh*
champagne	**champagne**	*shaN-pahny*
table wine	**vin ordinaire**	*vaiN or-dee-nair*
burgundy	**le bourgogne**	*boor-gony*
hock	**le vin du Rhin**	*vaiN d(ee) raiN*
port	**porto**	*por-toh*
madeira	**madère**	*mah-dair*
sherry	**Xérès**	*zay-rais*
beer (pale, dark)	**de la bière (blonde, brune)**	*byair (bloNd, br(ee)n)*
small glass of beer	**un bock**	*bock*
large glass of beer	**un demi**	*d'mee*
appetizer	**un apéritif**	*ah-pay-ree-teef*
cider	**le cidre**	*seedr*

cognac (brandy from the Cognac region)	cognac	kon-yahk
brandy	eau de vie	ohd-vee
sloe brandy	la prunelle	pr(ee)-nail
cider brandy	le calvados	kahl-vahdos
cherry brandy	le kirsch	keersh
white (grape) brandy	le marc	mahr
liqueur brandy	la fine champagne	feen-shaN-pahny
gin	le genièvre	zh-nyaivr
rum	le rhum	rom
liqueur	la liqueur	lee-k(ai)r
syrup	le sirop	see-roh

SHOPS AND SHOPPING

SHOPS AND SHOPPING	MAGASINS ET ACHATS	mah-gah-zaiN ay ah-shah
shop	le magasin	mah-gah-zaiN
departmental stores	les grands magasins	graN mah-gah-zaiN
to buy	acheter	ahsh-tay
to pay	payer	pay-yay
supermarket	le supermarché	s(ee)p-air-mahr-shay
cash-and-wrap	caisse et emballage	cays ait eN-bahl-ahzh
shoe department	le rayon de chaussures	rai-yóN de shoh-s(ee)r
shop window	la vitrine	veet-reen
showcase	la devanture	de-vaN-t(ee)r
salesman; shop assistant	le vendeur	vaN-d(ai)r
saleswoman	la vendeuse	vaN-d(ay)z
the sale	la vente	vaNt
price	le prix	pree
manager	le gérant	zhay-raN

What can I do for you Madam?	Madame désire . . .	mah-dahm day-zeer
I want to buy some soap	Je désire acheter du savon	zhe day-zee-rahsh-tay d(ee) sah-voN
Have you got any razor blades?	Avez-vous des lames?	ah-vay voo day lahm
How many do you require?	Combien en désirez-vous?	koN-by(ai)-aN day-zee-ray voo
A dozen. A pair	Une douzaine Une paire	(ee)n doo-zain:(ee)n pair
How much is it?	Combien est-ce?	koN-by(ai)-aise
It is too big	C'est trop grand	sai troh graN
small	petit	p'tee
thick	épais	ay-pai
thin	mince	maiNs
long	long	loN
short	court	koor
wide	large	lahrzh
narrow	étroit	ay-trwah
dear	cher	shair
Have you anything?	Avez-vous quelque chose?	ah-vay voo kailk shohz

bigger?	de plus grand?	*de pl(ee) graN*
smaller?	petit?	*p'tee*
dearer?	cher?	*shai,*
cheaper?	meilleur marché?	*mai-y(ai)r mahr-shay*

Something in	Quelque chose en	*kailk shohz aN*
silk	soie	*swah*
wool	laine	*lain*
cotton	coton	*koh-toN*
linen	toile	*twahl*
leather	cuir	*kweer*
metal	métal	*may-tahl*
I'll take it (them)	Je le (les) prendrai	*zhe le (lay) praN-dray*
Can you change this note?	Pouvez-vous changer ce billet?	*poo-vay voo shaN-zhay se bee-yay*
Please send it to this address	Veuillez l'envoyer à cette adresse	*v(ai)yay laN-vwah-yay ah sai-tahd-rais*

COLOURS   LES COULEURS   *koo-l(ai)r*

black	noir(e)	*nwahr*
blue	bleu(e)	*bl(ay)*

brown	brun(e)	br(ai)N; br(ee)n
chestnut	marron	mah-roN
cream	crème	kraim
dark	foncé(e)	foN-say
green	vert(e)	vair; vairt
grey	gris(e)	gree; greez
light	clair(e)	klair
mauve	mauve	mohv
pink	rose	rohz
red	rouge	roozh
white	blanc(he)	blaN; blaNsh
yellow	jaune	zhohn

BAKER	LE BOULANGER	le boo-laN-zhay
baker's shop	la boulangerie	lah-boo-laN-zh'ree
bread	du pain	d(ee) paiN
white bread	blanc	blaN
wholemeal (brown) bread	bis	bee
rye bread	de seigle	de saigle
new bread	frais	frai
stale bread	rassis	rah-see

a loaf	une miche	*meesh*
crescent-shaped rolls	des croissants	*krwah-saN*
rolls	des petits pains	*day p'tee paiN*
cake	le gâteau	*gah-toh*
bun	la brioche	*bree-osh*

BOOKSELLER	**LE LIBRAIRE**	*le leeb-rair*
bookshop	la librairie	*lah leeb-rai-ree*
book	le livre	*le leevr*
dictionary	le dictionnaire	*le deek-syoh-nair*
guide book	le guide	*le geed*
map	une carte	*kahrt*
hand-book	le manuel	*mah-n(ee)ail*
English novel	le roman anglais	*roh-maN aN-glai*
romance	l'histoire d'amour anglaise	*lees-twahr dahm-oor aNg-lais*

BANK	**LA BANQUE**	*baNk*
foreign exchange office	le bureau de change	*b(ee)-roh de shaNzh*
money	l'argent	*ahr-zhaN*
to change	changer	*shaN-zhay*

rate of exchange	le cours du change	koor d(ee) shaNzh
small change	la monnaie	mo-nai
bank note (hundred francs)	un billet (de cent francs)	bee-yai (de saN fraN)
ten-franc piece	une pièce de dix francs	pyais de dee fraN
American (Canadian) dollar	le dollar américain (canadien)	do-lahr ah-may-ree-kaiN (kah-nahd-yain)
pound (sterling)	la livre anglaise	leevr aN-glaiz
receipt	un reçu	re-s(ee)
I wish to change English (American) money	Pourrais-je changer ici de l'argent anglais (américain)	poo-rai-zhe shaN-zhay ee-see de lahr-zhaN aN-glai (ah-may-ree-kaiN)
to pay cash	payer comptant	pai-yay koN-taN
to draw money	toucher de l'argent	too-shay de lahr-zhaN
to cash a cheque	toucher un chèque	too-shay (ai)N shaik
to pay in bank notes	payer en billets	pay-yay an bee-yai
silver	monnaie	mo-nai
travellers' cheques	les chèques de voyage	shaik de vwah-yahzh
do you use the Euro-cheque system?	utilisez-vous les Euro-chèques?	(ee)t-eel-eez-ay voo lays (ee)roh-shaik

| do you take credit cards? | acceptez-vous les cartes de crédit | *ahk-saipt-ayvoolay kahrt de cray-dee* |

BOOTMAKER — LE CORDONNIER — *le kor-don-yay*

boots	les bottes	*lay bot*
shoes	les souliers	*lay sool-yay*
sandals	les sandales	*lay saN-dahl*
to mend	raccommoder	*rah-ko-mo-day*
to sole	mettre des semelles	*maitr day se-mail*
to heel	mettre des talons	*maitr day tah-loN*
high-heeled shoes	souliers à hauts talons	*sool-yay ah oh tah-loN*
low-heeled shoes	des souliers plats	*day sool-yay plah*
polish	le cirage	*see-rahzh*
laces	des lacets	*lah-say*

BUTCHER — LE BOUCHER — *le boo-shay*

| butcher's shop | la boucherie | *la boosh-ree* |
| meat | la viande | *la vyaNd* |

(For kinds of meat, see Food-list on page 88.)

CAMERA SHOP	LA BOUTIQUE DE PHOTOGRAPHE	*boo-teek de foh-toh-grahf*
black and white film	le film en noir et blanc	*feelm aN nwahr ai blaN*
35 mm film	le film en trente-cinq millimétres	*feelm aN traNt-siNk mee-lee-maitr*
colour film	le film en couleur	*feelm aN coo-l(ai)r*
cartridge film	le film à cartouche	*feelm ah cahr-toosh*
for slides	pour les diapositives	*poor lay dee-ah-pos-eet-eev*
for prints	pour les épreuves	*poor lays aip-r(ai)v*
fast film	le film rapide	*feelm rah-peed*
slow film	le film lent	*feelm laN*
can you develop this?	pouvez-vous dévelop-per ceci?	*poo-vay voo day-ve-lo-pay se-see*
can you load this camera (unload)	pouvez-vous charger (vider) cet appareil	*poo-vay voo shahr-zhay (vee-day) sait ahp-ahr-aiy*
flashgun	la lampe de flash	*laNp de flahsh*
flashbulb	l'ampoule de flash	*laN-pool de flahsh*
aperture	l'ouverture	*loov-airt-(ee)r*

lens	l'objectif	*lobzh-aik-teef*
shutter speed	le réglage de vitesse de	*ray-glahzh de vee-tais*
adjustment	l'obdurateur	*de lob-d(ee)r-aht-(ai)r*
negatives	les négatifs	*nay-gah-teef*
can you print this?	pouvez-vous tirer ceci?	*poo-vay voo tee-ray se-see*
can you enlarge this?	pouvez-vous agrandir ceci?	*poo-vay voo ahg-raN-deer se-see*
contact prints	les épreuves par contact	*lays ay-pr(ai)v pahr coN-tahkt*

(N.B. In French, camera can be translated in two ways appareil à photo (for still pictures) but caméra (cah-may-rah) for movie pictures)

CHEMIST	LE PARFUMEUR	*le pahr-f(ee)-m(ai)r*
(See also Dispensing Chemist)		
soap	du savon	*d(ee) sah-voN*
razor	un rasoir	*(ai)N rahz-wahr*
blade	une lame	*(ee)n lahm*
hair lotion	une lotion pour les cheveux	*lohs-yoN poor lay shv(ay)*

nail polisher	un polissoir	po-lees-wahr
nail polish	du vernis à ongles	d(ee) vair-nee ah zoNgl
shaving stick	un savon à barbe	sah-voN ah barb
lipstick	du rouge à lèvres	d(ee) roozh ah laivr
face powder	la poudre de riz	la poodr-de ree
scent; perfume	le parfum	le pahr-f(ai)N
eau de Cologne	eau de Cologne	ohd'ko-lony
cream	la crème de beauté	kraim de boh-tay
tooth brush	une brosse à dents	(ee)n bro-sah daN
tooth paste	la pâte dentifrice	paht daN-tee-frees

DISPENSING CHEMIST

LE PHARMACIEN   *fars-mahs-yaiN*

aspirin	aspirine	ahs-pee-reen
Vaseline	vaseline	vah-ze-leen
iodine	teinture d'iode	taiN-t(ee)r dee-ohd
bicarbonate of soda	du bicarbonate de soude	d(ee) bee-kahr-boh-naht-de sood
castor oil	de l'huile de ricin	de lweel d'ree-saiN
cotton wool	du coton	d(ee) koh-toN

laxative	un laxatif	lah-ksah-teef
purgative	un purgatif	p(ee)r-gah-teef
palliative (pain killer)	un anodin	ah-noh-daiN
antidote	un contre-poison	coNtr-pwah-zoN
bandage	un pansement	paNs-maN
sanitary towel	une serviette hygiénique	(ee)n sair-vyait eezh-yay-neek

CONFECTIONER'S LA CONFISERIE *lah koN-feez-ree*

chocolate	du chocolat	d(ee) shoh-koh-lah
sweets	des bonbons	day boN-boN
toffee	du caramel au beurre	kah-rah-mai-loh (b(ai)r
crystallised fruit	des fruits glacés	frwee glah-say
cream chocolate	du chocolat fourré	sho-koh-lah foo-ray
barley sugar	du sucre d'orge	d(ee) s(ee)kr dorzh
sugar almond	des dragées	drah-zhay

DAIRY	LA CRÈMERIE	*lah kraim'ree*
	LA LAITERIE	*lah lait-ree*
milk	du lait	*d(ee) lai*
butter	du beurre	*d(ee) b(ai)r*
eggs	des œufs	*day-z(ay)*
cheese	du fromage	*d(ee) fro-mahzh*
DRAPER	UN MARCHAND DE NOUVEAU- TÉS	*mahr-shaN de noo- voh-tay*
dress materials and silk goods	étoffes et soieries	*ay-tof ay swah-ree*
woollen stuffs	des lainages (m.pl.)	*day lai-nahzh*
underclothing	la lingerie	*laiNzh'ree*
DRESSMAKER	LE COUTURIER	*koo-t(ee)r-yay*
	LA COUTURIÈRE	*koo-t(ee)r-yair*
blouse	la blouse	*blooz*
coat, cloak, mantle	un manteau	*maN-toh*
evening	un manteau de soirée	*de swah-ray*

sports	un manteau de sport	de spor
tailor made	un costume tailleur	kos-t(ee)m tah-y(ai)r
jacket	la jaquette	zhah-kait
skirt	la jupe	zh(ee)p
dress, frock, gown	une robe	rob
afternoon	d'après-midi	dahp-rai mee-dee
dance	de danse	de daNs
evening	du soir	d(ee) swahr
walking	de ville	de veel
house	d'intérieur	d'iN-tayr-yair
sports	de sport	de spor
Mini skirt	La jupe mini	zh(ee)p mee-nee
Midi skirt	La jupe midi	zh(ee)p mee-dee
Maxi coat	Le manteau maxi	maN-toh mahk-si

DYERS AND CLEANERS — LA TEINTURERIE — tiN-t(ee)-re-ree

to clean	nettoyer	nait-wah-yay
to dye	teindre	tiNdr

ELECTRICAL SHOP	LE MAGASIN ÉLECTRIQUE	mah-gahz-iN ay-laik-treek
this is broken	ceci est cassé	se-see ai k ah-say
can you mend lt?	pouvez-vous le réparer?	poo-vay voo le ray-pah-ray
radio	la radio	radee-oh
television	la télévision	tay-lay-vee-zyoN
fan	le ventilateur	vaN-tee-lah-t(ai)r
heater	l'appareil de chauffage	lah-pah-raiy de shoh-fahzh
washing machine	la machine à laver	mah-sheen ah lah-vay
spin-drier	l'essoreuse-sécheuse	lais-or-(ai)z-say-sh(ai)z
electric mixer	le mixeur électrique	meek-s(ai)r ay-laik-treek
electric blender	le mélangeur électrique	may-laN-zh(ai)r ay-laik-treek
vacuum cleaner	l'aspirateur	lahs-peer-aht-(ai)r
electric light	la lumière électrique	l(ee)m-yair ay-laik-treek

electric oven	le four électrique	*foor ay-laik-treek*
stove	la cuisinière	*kwee-zeen-yair*
grill	le gril	*gree*
bell	la sonnette	*so-nait*
hotplate	le chauffe-plat	*shohf-plah*
switch	le bouton	*boo-toN*
time-switch	le commutateur à horlogerie	*kom-(ee)t-aht-(ai)r ah or-lozh'ree*
electric blanket	la couverture élec-trique	*coo-vair-t(ee)r ay-laik-treek*
refrigerator	le réfrigérateur	*ray-freezh-ay-rah-t(ai)r*
fuse	le fusible	*f(ee)-zeebl*
fuse-wire	le plomb à fusible	*ploN-ahf(ee)-zeebl*
light bulb	l'ampoule électrique	*laN-pool ay-laik-treek*
socket	la douille	*dwee*
5-amp plug	la prise de cinq ampères	*preez d'saiNk aNpair*
adaptor	la prise multiple	*preez m(ee)l-teepl*

FISHMONGER'S	LA POISSONNERIE	*lah-pwah-son-ree*
fish	un poisson	*aiN pwah-soN*

(See Food-list on page 88)

FRUITERER AND GREENCROCER	LE FRUITIER	*le frweet-yay*
fruit	des fruits	*day frwee*
vegetables	des légumes	*day lay-g(ee)m*

(See Food-list on page 88)

GROCER	L'ÉPICIER	*ay-pees-yay*

(See list on page 88.)

HAIRDRESSER	LE COIFFEUR	*le kwah-f(ai)r*
shave, please	la barbe, s'il vous plaît	*lah barb seel-voo-plai*
haircut, please	les cheveux, s'il vous plaît	*lay shv(ay) seel-voo-plai*
not too short	pas trop courts	*pah troh koor*
rather short	assez courts	*ah-say koor*

short behind and rather long in front	courts derrière et as-sez longs par devant	*koor dair-yair ay ah-say loN pahr de-vaN*
at the sides	aux côtés	*oh koh-tay*
water-wave	onduler à l'eau	*oN-d(ee)lay ah loh*
permanent wave	une permanente	*pair-mah-naNt*

HATTER	**LE CHAPELIER**	*shah-pe-lyay*
hat	un chapeau	*shah-poh*
felt	un feutre	*f(ai)tr*
bowler	un melon	*me-loN*
soft	un chapeau mou	*shah-poh moo*
straw	un chapeau de paille	*shah-poh de pahy*
top	un haut de forme	*oh d'form*
opera	un chapeau claque	*shah-poh klahk*
cap	une casquette	*kahs-kait*

| **HOSIER** | **LE CHEMISIER** (See list on page 177.) | *she-meez-yay* |

JEWELLER	LE BIJOUTIER	bee-zhoo-tyai
precious stones	des pierres précieuses (f.pl.)	pyair prays-y(ai)z
beads	des perles (f.pl.)	pairl
bracelet	bracelet (m.)	brahs-lay
brooch	broche (f.)	brosh
ear-ring	boucle d'oreille (f.)	bookl do-raiy
necklace	collier (m.)	kol-yay
pin	épingle (f.)	ay-piNgl
ring	bague (f.)	bahg
wedding ring	une alliance	ahl-yaNs
stud	un bouton	boo-toN
golden; silver	en or; en argent	aN-nor; aN-nahr-zhaN
platinum	platine (m.)	plah-teen
ivory	ivoire (m.)	eev-wahr
mother-of-pearl	nacre (f.)	nahkr
pearl	perle (f.)	pairl
string of pearls	un fil de perles	feel de pairl

LAUNDRY	LA BLANCHISSERIE	*lah blaN-shees-ree*
laundry-list	le carnet de linge	*kahr-nayd'liNzh*
shirt	la chemise	*sh'meez*
vest	le gilet de flanelle	*zhee-lay de flah-nail*
collar	un faux-col	*foh-kol*
drawers, pants	des caleçons	*kahl-soN*
socks	des chaussettes	*shoh-sait*
towel	une serviette de toilette	*sair-vyait de twah-let*
handkerchief	un mouchoir	*moosh-wahr*
stockings	les bas	*bah*
knickers	une culotte	*k(ee) lot*
skirt	la jupe	*zh(ee)p*
petticoat	le jupon	*zh(ee)-poN*
dressing-gown	le peignoir	*pain-ywahr*
nightdress	une chemise de nuit	*(ee)n shmeez de nwee*
pyjamas	le pyjama	*pee-zhah-mah*
blouse; overall	une blouse	*blooz*
camisole	un cache-corset	*kahsh-kor-sai*
chemise	une chemise	*sh'meez*
combinations	une combinaison	*koN-bee-naizoN*

corset	le corset	kor-sai
apron	un tablier	tahb-lyay
brassiere	un soutien-gorge	soot-yaiN gorzh

MILLINER — LA MODISTE — moh-deest

hat	un chapeau	(ai)N shah-po
felt	de feutre	de f(ai)tr
straw	de paille	de pahy
velvet	de velours	de ve-loor
with turned-up brim	relevé	re-le-vay
with wide brim	un capeline	kah-pe-leen

PASTRYCOOK — LE PATISSIER — pah-tees-yay

| the shop, pastry | la pâtisserie | pah-tees'ree |

(See Food-list on page 88)

PERFUMER — LE PARFUMEUR — pahr-f(ee)-m(ai)r

the trade, shop, scents	la parfumerie	pahr-f(ee)m're
a cake of toilet soap	un savon de toilette	sah-voN de twah-lait
scented with voilet	à la violette	ah-lah vyoh-lait

scented with eau de Cologne	à l'eau de Cologne	*ah lohd'ko-lony*
scented with milk of almonds	aux amandes amères	*ah-zah-maN-dah-mair*
eau de Cologne	l'eau de Cologne	*ohd-ko-lony*
lavender water	l'eau de lavande	*ohd-lah-vaNd*
perfume	le parfum	*pahr-f(ai)N*

STATIONER — LE PAPETIER — *le pah-pe-tyay*

stationer's	la papeterie	*pah-pet-ree*
pencil	un crayon	*krai-yoN*
pen-holder	un porte-plume	*port pl(ee)m*
nib	une plume	*pleem*
ball-point pen	le stylo à bille	*stee-loh ah bee*
refill	la recharge	*lah r'shahrzh*
paper	du papier	*pahp-yay*
notepaper	du papier à lettres	*pahp-yay ah laitr*
pad of writing paper	un bloc de papier	*blok de pahp-yay*
blotting paper	du papier buvard	*pahp-yay b(ee)vahr*
packing paper	du papier d'emballage	*pahp-yay daN bah-lahzh*

toilet paper	du papier hygiénique	*pahp-yay ee-zhyay-neek*
typewriting-paper	du papier machine	*pahp-yay mah-sheen*
envelope	une enveloppe	*aN-v'lop*

TAILOR — LE TAILLEUR — *tah-y(ai)r*

made to measure	fait sur measure	*fai s(ee)r me-z(ee)r*
ready-made	tout fait	*too fai*
lounge-suit	le complet veston	*koN-plai vais-toN*
dinner jacket	le smoking	*smoh-king*
evening dress	l'habit	*ah-bee*
jacket	le veston	*vais-toN*
waistcoat	le gilet	*zhee-lai*
trousers	le pantalon	*paN-tah-loN*
overcoat	le pardessus	*pahr-de s(ee)*

TOBACCONIST'S — LE BUREAU DE TABAC — *le b(ee)-roh de tah-bah*

tobacco	le tabac	*tah-bah*
a box of matches	une boîte d'allumettes	*bwaht dah-l(ee)-mait*
cigarettes	des cigarettes	*see-gah-rait*

a cigar	un cigare	*see-gahr*
pipe	la pipe	*peep*
lighter	un briquet	*bree-kay*

WATCHMAKER	UN HORLOGER	*or-lo-zhay*
watch	une montre	*moNtr*
wrist-watch	un bracelet-montre	*brahs-lay-moNtr*
clock	la pendule	*paN-d(ee)l*
alarm-clock	un réveil	*ray-vaiy*
to be fast	avancer	*ah-vaN-say*
to be slow	retarder	*re-tahr-day*
to wind up	remonter	*re-moN-tay*

THE WEATHER

THE WEATHER	LE TEMPS	*taN*
What sort of weather is it?	Quel temps fait-il?	*kail taN fai-teel*
The weather is fine (bad)	Il fait beau (mauvais)	*eel fai boh (moh-vai)*

It is hot	Il fait chaud	*eel fai shoh*
cold	froid	*frwah*
cool	frais	*frai*
freezing	Il gèle	*eel zhail*
thawing	Il dégèle	*eel day-zhail*
wet	Il fait humide	*eel fai (ee)-meed*
foggy	du brouillard	*d(ee) broo-yahr*
sunny	du soleil	*d(ee) so-laiy*
close	lourd	*loor*
dull	sombre	*soNbr*
windy	du vent	*d(ee) vaN*
stormy	Il y a une tempête	*eel yah (ee)n taN-pait*
raining	Il pleut	*eel pl(ay)*
snowing	Il neige	*eel naizh*
thundering	Il fait de l'orage	*eel fai de loh-rahzh*
lightning	des éclairs	*day zay-klair*
a flash of lightning	un coup de foudre	*koo de foodr*
There is a storm in the air	Il y a un orage dans l'air	*eel-yah (ai)-noh-rahzh daN lair*
The sky is overcast	Le ciel est couvert	*le syai-lai koo-vair*
clear	clair	*klair*

The air is fresh stifling	L'air est frais étouffant	*lai-rai frai ay-too-faN*
sunrise (sunset)	le lever (coucher) du soleil	*le-vay (koo-shay) d(ee) so-laiy*
It is moonlight	Il fait clair de lune	*eel fai klair de l(ee)n*
We shall have rain	Il va pleuvoir	*eel vah pl(ay)-vwahr*
a few drops of rain	quelques gouttes de pluie	*kailk goot de pl(w)ee*
a heavy shower	une averse	*ah-vairs*
It is pouring	Il pleut à verse	*eel pl(ay)-tah-vairs*
The streets are flooded	Les rues sont inondées	*lay r(ee) soN-tee-noN-day*
You will get wet	Vous allez être mouillé	*voo-zah-lay-zaitr moo-yay*
It has stopped raining	il a cessé de pleuvoir	*ee-lah sai-say de pl(ay)-vwahr*
rainbow	un arc-en-ciel	*ahr-kaN-syail*
high temperature	une haute température	*oht taN-pay-rah-t(ee)r*
mean temperature	une température moyenne	*taN-pay-rah-t(ee)r mwah-yain*
low temperature	une température basse	*taN-pay-rah-t(ee)r bahs*

The barometer	Le baromètre	*bah-roh-maitr*
is falling	descend	*dais-saN*
is rising	monte	*moNt*
is high	est haut	*ai-toh*
is low	est bas	*ai-bah*
indicates	est au	*ai-toh*
variable	variable	*vahr-yahbl*
The thermometer	Le thermomètre	*tair-moh-maitr*
above zero	au-dessus de zéro	*oh dai-s(ee) de zay-roh*
below zero	au-dessous de zéro	*oh dai-soo de zay-roh*
degree	le degré	*de-gray*
I am cold (hot)	J'ai froid (chaud)	*zhai frwah (shoh)*

THE THERMOMETER

THE THERMOMETER   LE THERMOMETRE *tair-moh-maitr*

Fahrenheit	Celsius
—4	—20
0	—17,8
5	—15
23	—5
32 freezing point	—0 point de congélation (zéro)
41	5
55	12,7
60	15,5
65	18,3
70	21,1
77	25
80	26,6
85	29,4
90	32,2
95	35

Fahrenheit	Celsius
100	37,7
113	45
176	80
212 boiling point	100 point d'ébullition

Note.—On the Continent the Celsius (= Centigrade) scale is employed.

To turn Fahrenheit into Celsius, subtract 32 and multiply by $\frac{5}{9}$; e.g.:

$$95°F. = (95-32) \times \frac{5}{9} = 35°C.$$

To turn Celsius into Fahrenheit, multiply by $\frac{9}{5}$ and add 32; e.g.

$$-5°C. = (-5 \times \frac{9}{5}) + 32 = 23°F.$$

TIME AND DATE

DIVISIONS OF TIME	DIVISIONS DU TEMPS	*dee-veez-yoNd(ee)taN*
second	la seconde	*s'goNd*
minute	la minute	*mee-n(ee)t*

hour	une heure	(ai)r
quarter of an hour	une demi-heure	de-mee (ai)r
quarter of an hour	un quart d'heure	kahr d(ai)r
day	le jour; la journée[1]	zhoor; zhoor-nay
week	la semaine; huit jours	s'main; (w)ee zhoor
fortnight	quinze jours	kaiNz zhoor
month	le mois	mwah
year	une année; un an	ah-nay; aN
century	le siècle	syaikl
dawn	la pointe du jour; l'aube	pwiNt d(ee) zhoor; ohb
morning	le matin	mah-tiN
forenoon	la matinée	mah-tee-nay
noon	midi	mee-dee
afternoon	une après-midi	ah-prai-mee-dee
evening	le soir	swahr
dusk	le crépuscule	kray-p(ee)s-k(ee)l
night	la nuit	nwee
midnight	minuit	mee-nwee
a.m.	avant midi	ah-vaN mee-dee

1 Whole day in regard to work

p.m.	après-midi	*ah-prai mee-dee*
in the course of the day	dans la journée	*daN lah zhoor-nay*

THE DAYS OF THE WEEK
LES JOURS DE LA SEMAINE
lay zhoor de lah s'main

Monday	lundi	*l(ai)N-dee*
Tuesday	mardi	*mahr-dee*
Wednesday	mercredi	*mairkr'dee*
Thursday	jeudi	*zh(ay)-dee*
Friday	vendredi	*vaNdr'dee*
Saturday	samedi	*sahm-dee*
Sunday	dimanche	*dee-maNsh*

MONTHS
LES MOIS
mwah

January	janvier	*zhaN-vyay*
February	février	*fayv-ree-ay*
March	mars	*mahrs*
April	avril	*ahv-reel*
May	mai	*mai*
June	juin	*zhwaiN*

July	**juillet**	*zhwee-yay*
August	**août**	*oo*
September	**septembre**	*saip-taNbr*
October	**octobre**	*ok-tobr*
November	**novembre**	*noh-vaNbr*
December	**décembre**	*day-saNbr*

THE SEASONS	LES SAISONS	*sai-soN*
Spring	**le printemps**	*priN-taN*
Summer	**l'été (m.)**	*ay-tay*
Autumn	**l'automne (m.)**	*oh-ton*
Winter	**l'hiver (m.)**	*ee-vair*
in spring	**au printemps**	*oh praiN-taN*
in summer	**en été**	*aN-nay-tay*
in autumn	**en automne**	*aN-noh-ton*
in winter	**en hiver**	*aN-nee-vair*
What is to-day's date?	**Quelle date sommes-nous aujourd'hui?**	*kail daht som noo-zoh zhoor-dwee*
the 1st of January	**le premier janvier**	*prem-yay zhaN-vyay*
the 2nd of February	**le deux février**	*d(ay) fayv-ree-ay*
the 3rd of March	**le trois mars**	*trwah mahrs*

THE PAST	LE PASSÉ	*pah-say*
yesterday	hier	*yair*
the day before yesterday	avant-hier	*ah-vaNt yair*
this day last week	il y a aujourd'hui huit jours	*eel-yah oh-zhoor-dwee wee zhoor*
this day last year	il y a un an	*eel-yah (ai)naN*
an hour ago	il y a une heure	*eel-yah (ee)n (ai)r*
two days ago	deux jours	*d(ay) zhoor*
three weeks ago	trois semaines	*trwah s'main*
last Friday	vendredi dernier	*vaNdr'dee dairn-yay*
last week	la semaine dernière	*s'main dairn-yair*
this morning	ce matin	*se mah-taiN*
last night	hier soir	*yair swahr*
lately; recently	récemment	*ray-sah-maN*
a little while ago; just now	tantôt; tout à l'heure	*taN-toh; too-tah-l(ai)r*

THE PRESENT	LE PRÉSENT	*pray-zaN*
to-day	aujourd'hui	*oh-zhoord-wee*
now; at present	maintenant	*maiNt-naN*

nowadays	de nos jours	de noh zhoor
in time	à temps	ah taN
It is late	Il est tard	ee-lai tahr
I am late	je suis en retard	zhe swee-zaN re-tahr
early	de bonne heure	de bo-n(ai)r
a little while	un petit moment	p'tee moh-maN
a long time	longtemps	loN-taN
for the present; temporarily	provisoirement	proh-vee-zwahr-maN

| THE FUTURE | L'AVENIR | ahv'neer |

to-morrow	demain	d'maiN
the day after to-morrow	après-demain	ah-prai d'maiN
immediately	immédiatement	eè-mayd-yaht-maN
soon	bientôt	byaiN-toh
directly	tout de suite	tood-sweet
presently	tout à l'heure	too-tah-l(ai)r
later on	plus tard	pl(ee) tahr
next Monday	lundi prochain	l(ai)N-dee pro-sh(ai)N
next week	la semaine prochaine	s'main pro-shain

next year	l'année (f.) prochaine	ah-nay pro-shain
this afternoon	cette après-midi	sai-tah-prai mee-dee
this evening (to-night)	ce soir	se swahr
in a few days	dans quelques jours	daN kailk zhoor
a week today	aujourd'hui en huit	oh-zhoord-wee aN-weet
in a fortnight	dans une quinzaine	daN-z(ee)n kaiN-zain
in a short while	en peu de temps	aN p(ay) de taN
within (after) five minutes	en (dans) cinq minutes	aN (daN) saiN mee-n(ee)t
a long time	longtemps	loN-taN
a short while	peu de temps	p(ay) de taN
for good	pour toujours	poor too-zhoor

HOW OFTEN	**COMBIEN DE FOIS**	*koN-byaiN de fwah*
sometimes	quelquefois	kailk-fwah
often	souvent	soo-vaN
always	toujours	too-zhoor
frequently	fréquemment	fray-kah-maN
constantly	continuellement	koN-tee-n(ee)-ail-maN
rarely	rarement	rahr'maN
never	jamais	zhah-mai

every day	tous les jours	*too lay zhoor*
twice a day	deux fois par jour	*d(ay) fwah pahr zhoor*
three times a week	trois fois par semaine	*trwah fwah pahr s'main*
so often	tant de fois	*taN de fwah*
now and then	de temps en temps	*de-taN-zaN taN*

TIME — L'HEURE — *l(ai)r*

What time is it?	Quelle heure est-il?	*kai-l(ai)rai-teel*
It is nearly four o'clock	Il est presque quatre heures	*ee-lai praisk' kahtr(ai)r*
It is exactly two o'clock	Il est juste deux heures	*ee-lai zh(ee)st d(ay)-z(ai)r*
It is about three o'clock	Il est environ trois heures	*ee-lai-taN-vee-roN trwah-z(ai)r*
It is five minutes past three	Il est trois heures cinq	*ee-lai trwah-z(ai)r siNk*
It is a quarter past six	Il est six heures et quart	*ee-lai see-z-(ai)-ray kahr*
It is half-past seven	Il est sept heures et demie	*ee-lai sai-t(ai)r ay d'mee*

It is twenty to eight	Il est huit heures moins vingt	ee-lai wee-t(ai)r mwaiN vaiN
It is a quarter to ten	Il est dix heures moins le quart	ee-lai dee-z(air) mwaiN le kahr
It is five to eleven	Il est onze heures moins cinq	ee-lai oN-z(ai)r mwaiN saiNk
It is noon	Il est midi	ee-lai mee-dee
It is midnight	Il est minuit	ee-lai meen-wee
It is ten past twelve (a.m.)	Il est minuit dix	ee-lai meen-wee dees
It is half-past twelve (p.m.)	Il est midi et demi	ee-lai mee-dee ay d'mee
shortly before (after) nine	quelques minutes avant (après) neuf heures	kailk mee-n(ee)t ah-vaN (ah-prai) n(ai)v(ai)r
six a.m.	six heures du matin	see-z(ai)r d(ee) mah-taiN
p.m.	du soir	d(ee) swahr
towards three p.m.	vers trois heures de l'après-midi	vair trwah-z(ai)r de lahp-rai mee-dee
four o'clock in the morning	quatre heures du matin	kaht-r(ai)r d(ee) mah-taiN

eleven o'clock a.m.	**onze heures du matin**	*oN-z(ai)r d(ee) mah-taiN*
the watch	**la montre**	*moNtr*
the clock	**l'horloge** (f.)	*or-lozh*
It is right	**Elle est à l'heure**	*ail ai-tah l(ai)r*
wrong	**n'est pas à l'heure**	*nai pah-zah l(ai)r*
fast	**Elle avance**	*ail ahvaNs*
slow	**retarde**	*re-tahrd*
It has stopped	**Elle est arrêtée**	*ai-lai-tah-rai-tay*
It has to be wound up	**Il faut la remonter**	*eel foh lah re-moN-tay*
repaired	**réparer**	*ray-pah-ray*
cleaned	**nettoyer**	*nait-wah-yay*

THE FAMILY

THE FAMILY	**LA FAMILLE**	*fah-meey*
Christian name	**le prénom**	*pray-noN*
surname	**le nom de famille**	*noN de fah-meey*
the parents	**les parents**	*pah-raN*

relative	le parent	*pah-raN*
near relation	proche parent	*prosh pah-raN*
distant relation	parent éloigné	*pah-raN tay-lwahn-yay*
parents-in-law	les beaux-parents	*boh pah-raN*
father	le père	*pair*
father-in-law	le beau-père	*boh-pair*
mother	la mère	*mair*
mother-in-law	la belle-mère	*bail-mair*
child	un (une) enfant	*aN-faN*
son	le fils	*fees*
daughter	la fille	*feey*
son-in-law	le beau-fils	*boh-fees*
daughter-in-law	la belle-fille	*bail-feey*
brother	le frère	*frair*
sister	la sœur	*s(ai)r*
half-brother	le demi-frère	*d'mee frair*
half-sister	la demi-sœur	*d'mee s(ai)r*
grandparents	les grands-parents	*graN pah-raN*
grandfather	le grand-père	*graN-pair*
grandmother	la grand-mère	*graN-mair*
grandson	le petit-fils	*p'tee-fees*

granddaughter	la petite-fille	p'teet-feey
cousin (male)	le cousin	coo-zaiN
cousin (female)	la cousine	coo-zeen
uncle	l'oncle	oN-kl
aunt	la tante	taNt
nephew	le neveu	n'v(ay)
niece	la nièce	nyais
born	né	nay
birth	la naissance	nai-saNs
birthday	l'anniversaire	ah-nee-vair-sair
French by birth	français de naissance	fraN-sai de nai-saNs
baptism	le baptême	bah-taim
baptised	baptisé	bah-tee-zay
godfather	le parrain	pah-raiN
godmother	la marraine	mah-rain
baby	le bébé	bay-bay
infant	le petit enfant	p'tee-taN-faN
(little) boy	le petit garçon	p'tee gahr-soN
(little) girl	la petite fille	p'teet feey
young man	le jeune homme	zh(ai)-nom
young woman	la jeune fille	zh(ai)n-feey
unmarried	célibataire	say-lee-bah-tair

engaged	fiancé	*fee-aN-say*
married	marié	*mahr-yay*
husband	le mari	*mah-ree*
wife	la femme	*fahm*

THE BODY

THE BODY	LE CORPS	*le kor*
hair	les cheveux	*sh'v(ay)*
head	la tête	*tait*
forehead	le front	*froN*
face	la figure; le visage	*fee-g(ee)r; vee-zahzh*
complexion	le teint	*taiN*
ear	une oreille	*oh-r(ai)y*
eye(s)	un œil; les yeux	*(ai)y; y(ay)*
eyebrow	le sourcil	*soor-see*
eyelash	le cil	*seel*
eyelid	la paupière	*poh-pyair*
nose	le nez	*nay*

mouth	la bouche	*boosh*
tongue	la langue	*laNg*
lip	la lèvre	*laivr*
cheek	la joue	*zhoo*
skin	la peau	*poh*
chin	le menton	*maN-toN*
beard	la barbe	*bahrb*
moustache	la moustache	*moos-tahsh*
neck	le cou	*koo*
shoulder	une épaule	*ay-poll*
chest; breast	la poitrine	*pwaht-reen*
heart	le cœur	*k(ai)r*
arm	le bras	*brah*
elbow	le coude	*kood*
stomach	l'estomac	*ais-toh-mah*
back	le dos	*doh*
hand	la main	*maiN*
thumb	le pouce	*poos*
finger	le doigt	*dwah*
waist	la taille	*tahy*
leg	la jambe	*zhaNb*
knee	le genou	*zh'noo*

foot	le pied	*pyay*
toes	les orteils	*or-taiy*
blood	le sang	*saN*
bald	chauve	*shohv*
blind	aveugle	*ah-v(ai)gl*
deaf	sourd	*soor*
dumb	muet	*m(ee)-ai*
crippled	estropié	*ais-troh-pyay*
humpbacked	bossu	*bo-s(ee)*
slim	mince	*maiNs*
stout	corpulent	*kor-p(ee)-laN*
young	jeune	*zh(ai)n*
old	vieux; vieille	*vy(ay); vyaiy*
tall	grand	*graN*
small	petit	*p'tee*
middle sized	de taille moyenne	*de tahy mwah-yain*
He is thirty years old	Il a trente ans	*ee-lah traN-taN*
How old is she?	Quel âge a-t-elle?	*kai-lahzh ah-tail*
How old are you?	Quel âge avez-vous?	*kai-lahzh ah-vay voo*
She has a nice figure	Elle est bien faite	*ai-lai byaiN fait*
good looking	beau (m.); belle (f.)	*boh; bail*
ugly	laid (m.); laide (f.)	*lai; laid*

Your health! (to somebody sneezing)	Que Dieu vous bénisse!	ke dy(ay) voo bay-nees
voice	la voix	vwah
to speak	parler	pahr-lay
to whisper	chuchoter	sh(ee)-shoh-tay
to call	appeler	ahp-lay
to shout	crier	kree-ay
to weep	pleurer	pl(ai)-ray
to sing	chanter	shaN-tay
to swallow	avaler	ah-vah-lay

HEALTH	LA SANTÉ	saN-tay
How are you?	Comment allez-vous?	ko-maN-tah-lay voo
How is your father?	Comment va Monsieur votre père?	ko-maN vah miss-y(ay) votr pair
Very well, thank you	Très bien, merci	trai byaiN mair-see
quite well	assez bien	ah-say byaiN
all right	pas trop mal	pah troh mahl
tolerably	passablement	pah-sahb-le-maN
not too well	pas trop bien	pah troh byaiN
You look well	Vous avez bonne mine	voo-zah-vay bon meen

| Are you not well? | N'allez-vous pas bien? | nah-lay voo pah byaiN |
| What is the matter with you? | Qu'avez-vous? | kah-vay voo |

SPORT

SPORT	LE SPORT	spor
to play tennis (golf, etc.)	jouer au tennis (golf, etc.)	zhoo-ay oh tai-nees (golf)
a game of ...	une partie de ...	(ee)n pahr-tee de
team; crew	une équipe	ay-keep
event; race	une épreuve	ay-pr(ai)v
heat	une épreuve élimina-toire	ay-pr(ai)v ay-lee-mee-nah-twahr
semi-final	une demi-finale	d'mee fee-nahl
final	une finale	fee-nahl
half-time	mi-temps	mee-taN
second half	la deuxième mi-temps	d(ay)z-yaim mee-taN
referee	un arbitre	ahr-beetr
spectator	un spectateur	spaik-tah-t(ai)r

ground	le terrain	*tai-raiN*
handicap	un handicap	*aN-dee-kahp*
penalty	une pénalité	*pay-nah-lee-tay*
disqualify	disqualifier	*dees-kah-leef-yay*
to win (won)	gagner (gagné)	*gahn-yay*
to lose (lost)	perdre (perdu)	*pairdr; pair-d(ee)*
to beat (beaten)	battre (battu)	*bahtr; bah-t(ee)*
athletics	l'athlétisme (m.)	*aht-lay-teezm*

| ATHLETICS | L'ATHLÉTISM | *laht-lay-teesm* |

putting the shot	poter le coup	*poh-tay le koo*
the high jump	le saut en hauteur	*soht aN-oh-t(ai)r*
pole vault	le saut à la perche	*soht ah lah pairsh*
long jump	le saut en longueur	*soht aN loN-g(ai)r*
throwing the hammer	jeter(lancer) le marteau	*zhe-tay (laN-say) le mahr-toh*
discus	le disque	*deesk*
javelin	le javelot	*zhav'loh*
world record	le record mondial	*re-kor moN-dyahl*

BOXING	LA BOXE	*boks*
a boxer	un boxeur	*bok-s(ai)r*
to knock out	metre k.o.	*maitr kah.oh*
to beat on points	battre aux points	*baht-roh pw(ai)N*
fly-weight	un poids mouche	*pwah moosh*
bantam-weight	un poids coq	*pwah kok*
feather-weight	un poids plume	*pwah pl(ee)m*
light-weight	un poids léger	*pwah lay-zhay*
welter-weight	un poids welter	*pwah wel-tair*
light middle-weight	un poids mi-moyen	*pwah mee-mwah-yaiN*
middle-weight	un poids moyen	*pwah mwah-yaiN*
heavy-weight	un poids lourd	*pwah loor*
a swing	un coup balancé	*koo bah-laN-say*
a straight left	un direct du gauche	*dee-raikt d(ee) gohsh*
a right hook	un crochet du droit	*kro-shai d(ee) drwah*
a low (foul) punch	un coup bas	*koo-bah*

BOATING	LE CANOTAGE	*kah-noh-tahzh*
rowing boat	un canot	*kah-noh*
oar	une rame	*rahm*
sailing boat	un bateau à voiles	*bah-toh ah vwahl*
sail	une voile	*vwahl*

CYCLING	LE CYCLISME	*see-kleezm*
to cycle	faire de la bicylette	*fair de 'lah bee-seek-lait*
FENCING	L'ESCRIME (f.)	*ais-kreem*
FISHING	LA PÊCHE	*paish*
angling	la pêche à la ligne	*pai-shah lah leeny*
to fish	pêcher	*pai-shay*
fishing-rod	une canne (à pêche)	*kahn ah paish*
line	la ligne	*leeny*
fish hook	un hameçon	*ahm-soN*
bait	l'appât (m.	*ah-pah*
FOOTBALL	LE FOOTBALL	*foot-bahl*
association football	l'assoce	*ah-sos*
rugby football	le rugby	*r(ee)g-bee*
goal	le but	*b(ee)*
ball	la balle	*bahl*
a run	une course	*koors*
a pass	une passe	*pahs*
a tackle	le plaquage	*plah kahzh*
a free kick	un coup franc	*koo fraN*

a throw-in	une remise en jeu	re-mee-zaN zh(ay)
to be off-side	être hors jeu	aitr or zh(ay)
goal-keeper	le gardien de but	gahr-dyaiN de b(ee)
forward	un avant	ah-vaN
back	un arrière	ahr-yair
half-back	un demi gauche	d'mee gohsh
outside (wing)	un ailier	ail-yay
inside right (left)	un inter droit (gauche)	aiN-tair drwah (gohsh)
centre forward	l'avant-centre	ah-vaN saNtr
goal post	le poteau	po-toh
free kick	le coup franc	koo fraN
three-quarter	un trois-quart	trwah-kahr
scrum	la mêlée	m(ai)-lay
try	un essai	ai-sai
line	la ligne	leeny
kick out	un renvoi	raN-vwah

| GAME SHOOTING | LA CHASSE | shahs |

GOLF	LE GOLF	golf
golf-course	un terrain de golf	tai-raiN de golf
golf-club	la canne	kahn

GYMNASTICS	LA GYMNASTIQUE	zheem-nahs-teek
HUNTING	LA CHASSE	shahs
HOCKEY	LE HOCKEY	o-kay
RACING (HORSE-)	LES COURSES DE CHEVAUX	koors de sh'voh
racecourse	un champ de course	shaN de koors
a race	une épreuve	ay-pr(ai)v
a flat race	une course plate	koors plaht
an obstacle race	une course d'obstacles	koors dobs -tahkl
the stands	les tribunes	tre-be(ee)n
the paddock	le pesage	pe-zahzh
the public enclosures	la pelouse	pe-looz
tip	un tuyau	t(ee)-yoh
to bet	parier	pahr-yay
to back ...	jouer ...	zhoo-ay
bookmaker	un bookmaker	book-mak-k(ai)r
totalisator	le totalisateur	toh-tah-lee-zah-t(ai)r
starting-point	le départ	day-pahr

finish	l'arrivée	ah-ree-vay
winner	le gagnant	gahn-yaN
RIDING	**MONTER A CHEVAL**	*moN-tay ah sh'vahl*
SHOOTING	**LE TIR**	*teer*
SKATING	**LE PATINAGE**	*pah-tee-nahzh*
to skate	patiner	*pah-tee-nay*
SKI-ING	**LE SKI**	*skee*
skis	des skis	*day skee*
ski boots	des bottes de ski	*day bot de skee*
ski sticks	des bâtons de ski	*day bah-toN de skee*
ski-lift	le remonte-pente	*le re-moNt paNt*
goggles	des lunettes protectrices	*day l(ee)nait prohtek-trees*
spring-board	le tremplin	*traN-plaiN*
downward run	la descente	*dais-saNt*
dangerously steep hill	descente dangereuse	*dais-saNt daN-zher-r(ai)z*

SWIMMING	LA NATATION	*nah-tah-syoN*
to swim	nager	*nah-zhay*
freestyle	le style libre	*steel leebr*
breast stroke	la brasse	*brahs*
butterfly	la nage papillon	*nahzh pah-pee-yon*
back stroke	la nage sur le dos	*nahzh s(ee)r le doh*
diving	plonger	*ploN -zhay*

TENNIS	LE TENNIS	*tai-nees*
tournament	le tournoi	*toor-nwah*
tennis-court	le court de tennis	*kòor de tai-nees*
ball	la balle	*bahl*
net	le filet	*fee-lay*
racket	la raquette	*rah-kait*
advantage	un avantage	*ah-vaN-tahzh*
forehand-drive	le coup droit	*koo drwah*
backhand	le revers	*re-vair*
service	le service	*sair-vees*
a fast service	un service canon	*sair-vees kah-noN*
deuce	égalité	*ay-gah-lee-tay*
two one	deux un	*d(ay) (ai)N*
two all	deux partout	*d(ay) pahr-too*

to lob	lobber	*lo-bay*
Whose advantage?	Avantage pour qui?	*ah-vaN-tahzh poor kee*
That's game	Ça fait jeu	*sah fai zh(ay)*
It is not up	J'ai doublé	*zhay doob-lay*
forty-fifteen	quarante-quinze	*kah-raNt-kaiNz*

| WATER-SKI-ING | LE SKI NAUTIQUE | *skee noh-teek* |
| to cross the wash | traverser le sillage | *trah-vair-say le see-yahzh* |

AMUSEMENTS

AMUSEMENTS	LES DISTRAC-TIONS	*dees-traks-yoN*
SHOWS	LES SPECTACLES	*spaik-tahkl*
theatre	le théâtre	*tay-ahtr*
opera	un opéra	*oh pay-rah*
light opera	opéra comique	*oh-pay-rah ko-meek*
musical comedy	une opérette	*oh-pay-rait*
music hall	le théâtre des variétés	*tay-ahtr day vahr-yay-tay*
concert	le concert	*koN-sair*

cinema	le cinéma	*see-nay-mah*
Punch and Judy	le Guignol	*geen-yol*
box office	le bureau de location	*b(ee)-roh de loh-kahs-yoN*
to book a seat	retenir une place	*re-te-neer (ee)n plahs*
ticket	le billet	*bee-yai*
programme	le programme	*proh-grahm*
opera glasses	des jumelles (f.pl.) de théâtre	*zh(ee)-mail de tay-ahtr*
cloak-room	le vestiaire	*vaist-yair*
a box	une loge	*lozh*
stage-box	une loge d'avant-scène	*dah-vaN sain*
front row of boxes	les premières loges	*prem-yair lozh*
front box	une loge de face	*de fahs*
side box	une loge de côté	*de koh-tay*
box below dress circle	une baignoire	*bain-ywahr*
dress circle	fauteuils de balcon	*foh-t(ai)y de bahl-koN*
orchestra stalls	fauteuils d'orchestre	*foh-t(ai)y dor-kaistr*
a seat in the stalls	un fauteuil	*foh-t(ai)y*
pit	le parterre	*pahr-tair*

balcony	le balcon	*bahl-koN*
gallery	l'amphithéâtre	*aN-fee-tay-ahtr*
a folding seat in a gangway	un strapontin	*strah-poN-tiN*
upper gallery; "the gods"	le poulailler; le paradis	*poo-lah-yay; par-rah-dee*
promenade (music hall)	le promenoir	*pro-men-wahr*
interval	l'entr'acte	*aN-trakt*

DANCING	LA DANSE	*daNs*
to dance	danser	*daN-say*
a dance	une danse; un bal	*daNs; bahl*
dance hall	un dancing; une salle de danse	*dahn-sing; sahl de daNs*
Are you fond of dancing?	Aimez-vous la danse?	*ai-may voo lah daNs*
May I have this waltz?	Voulez-vous m'accorder cette valse?	*voo-lay voo mah-kor-day sait vahls*

CASINO	LE CASINO	*kah-zee-noh*
gaming room	la salle de jeu	*sahl de zh(ay)*
cash-desk	la caisse	*kais*

counter	le jeton	zhe-toN
to ask in one's counters	toucher les jetons	too-shay lay zhe-toN
Put down your stakes	Faites vos jeux	fait voh zh(ay)
No more stakes can be placed	Rien ne va plus	ryaiN ne vah pl(ee)
even money chances	chance simple	shaNs saiNpl
varying odds	chance multiple	shaNs m(ee)l-teepl
all the red numbers	rouge	roozh
all the black numbers	noir	nwahr
all the even numbers	pair	pair
all the odd numbers	impair	iN-pair
all the numbers from 1 to 18	manque	maNk
all the numbers from 19 to 36	passe	pahs
the first twelve (1 to 12) numbers	première douzaine (P)	pre-myair doo-zaiN
the middle twelve numbers (13 to 24)	milieu (M)	meel-yay
the last twelve numbers (25 to 36)	dernière douzaine (D)	dairn-yair doo-zaiu

a single number	en plein	aN plaiN
two adjoining numbers	à cheval	ah sh'vahl
four adjoining numbers	en carré	aN kah-ray
0, 1, 2 and 3	quatre premiers	kahtr prem-yay

The above are some of the many variations possible in Roulette. There are thirty-six numbers, half of them red, half black, in addition to a 'zero.' 'Boule' is a simpler form of Roulette, with nine numbers only, in addition to a 'zero.'

PASTIMES

PASTIMES	PASSE-TEMPS (m.)	pahs-taN
Are you fond of . . .?	Aimez-vous . . .?	ai-may voo
music	la musique	m(ee)-zeek
singing	le chant	shaN
painting	la peinture	paiN-t(ee)r
drawing	le dessin	dai-saiN
sculpture	la sculpture	sk(ee)l-t(ee)r
skating	le patinage	pah-tee-nazh
dancing	la danse	daNs

gambling	**le jeu**	*zh(ay)*
the wireless	**la T.S.F. (télégra-phie sans fil)**	*tay-ais-aif*
Do you play . . . ?	**Jouez-vous . . . ?**	*zhoo-ay voo*
the piano	**du piano**	*d(ee) pee-ah-noh*
the violin	**du violon**	*d(ee) vee-oh-loN*
cards	**aux cartes**	*oh kahrt*
chess	**aux échecs**	*oh-zayh-shaik*
draughts	**aux dames**	*oh dahm*
billiards	**au billard**	*oh bee-yahr*
backgammon	**au jaquet**	*oh zhah-kai*

A GAME OF CHESS UNE PARTIE D'ECHECS *pahr-tee day-shaik*

chess board	**l'échiquier**	*ay-sheek-yay*
king	**le roi**	*rwah*
queen	**la reine**	*rain*
knight	**le cavalier**	*kah-vahl-yay*
rook	**la tour**	*toor*
bishop	**le fou**	*foo*
pawn	**le pion**	*py-oN*

to castle	roquer	ro-kay
check (to the king)	échec (au roi)	ay-shaik (oh rwah)
checkmate	échec et mat	ay-shaik ay maht

BILLIARDS	**LE BILLARD**	*bee-yahr*
billiard-table	le billard	*bee-yahr*
a cue	une queue	*k(ay)*
a ball	une bille	*bee-y*
cushions	les bandes	*baNd*
to cannon	faire un carambolage	*fair (ai)N kah-raN-boh-lahzh*

CARDS	**LES CARTES**	*kahrt*
What games do you play?	A quels jeux jouez-vous?	*ah kail zh(ay) zhoo-ay-voo*
bridge	le bridge	*breedzh*
poker	le poker	*poh-kair*
piquet	le piquet	*pee-kai*
whist	le whist	*weest*
to work out a patience	faire une patience	*fair (ee)n pahs-yaNs*
pack of cards	un jeu de cartes	*zh(ay)-de kahrt*

ace of spades	l'as de pique	*ahs de peek*
king of clubs	le roi de trèfle	*rwah de traifl*
queen of hearts	la dame de cœur	*dahm de k(ai)r*
knight of diamonds	le valet de carreau	*vah-lay de kah-roh*
ten of spades	dix de pique	*dees de peek*
nine of clubs	neuf de trèfle	*n(ai)f de traifl*
a game of bridge	une partie de bridge	*pahr-tee de breedzh*
(auction bridge)	(bridge aux enchères)	*breedzhoh-zaN-shair*
(contract bridge)	(bridge plafond)	*breedzh plah-foN*
to shuffle (shuffled)	battre (battu)	*bahtr; bah-t(ee)*
to cut	couper	*koo-pay*
whose deal?	à qui de donner?	*ah kee de do-nay*
whose lead?	à qui de jouer?	*ah kee de zhoo-ay*
partner	le partenaire	*pahrt-nair*
trump	l'atout (m.)	*ah-too*
no-trumps	sans-atout	*saN-zah-too*
trick	la levée	*le-vay*
to call	dire	*deer*
to double	doubler	*doob-lay*
to redouble	redoubler	*re-doo-blay*
to pass	passer	*pah-say*

suit	la couleur	koo-l(ai)r
to follow suit	jouer dans la couleur	zhoo-ay daN lah koo-l(ai)r
dummy	le mort	mor
to trump	couper	koo-pay
honours	les honneurs	o-n(ai)r

EMERGENCIES

EMERGENCY	URGENCE	(ee)r-zhaNs
Illness	maladie	mah-lah-dee
heart attack	crise cardiaque	kreez kahr-dyahk
he has collapsed	il s'est effondré	eel sayt ai-foN-dray
appendicitis	l'appendicite	lahp-aN-dee-ceet
he has stopped breathing	sa respiration s'est arrêtée	sah ray-speer-ah syoN sayt ahr-ait-ay
he has fainted	il s'est trouvé mal	eel say troo-vay mahl
he has been poisoned with this	il a été empoisonné par ceci	eel ah ayt-ay aNpwa-zo-nay pahr se-see

he has taken an overdose of this	il a trop pris de ceci	*eel ah troh pree de se-see*
he has a high temperature	il a beaucoup de fièvre	*eel ah boh-koo de fee-aivre*
The baby is arriving	le bébé est en train de naître	*le bay-bay ayt-aN traiN d'naitr*
He is having a fit	il a une crise	*eel ah (ee)n kreez*

ACCIDENTS	LES ACCIDENTS	*Layz ahk-see-daN*
There has been an accident	il y a eu un accident	*eel ee ah (ee) (ai)N ahk-see-daN*
the car (bus, plane, train) has crashed	la voiture (le car, l'avion, le train) a eu un accident	*lah vwah-t(ee)r (le cahr, lah-vyoN, le traiN) ah (ee) (ai)N ahk-see-daN*
he has broken his arm (leg)	il s'est cassé le bras (la jambe)	*eel say kah-say le brah (la zhaNb)*
he has been seriousiy injured	il est sérieusement b essé	*eel ay say-ry(ai)z-maN blai-say*
he is being swept out to sea	il a été emporté vers le large	*eel ah ayt-ay aN-portay vair le larzh*
he is drowning	il se noie	*eel se nwah*

the boat has capsized	le bateau s'est retourné	le bah-toh say re-toor-nay
man overboard	un homme à la mer	(ai)N om ah lah mair
he has fallen down the mountain (cliff)	il est tombé de la montagne (falaise)	eel ay toNbay de lah moNt-ahny (fahlays)
he has had an electric shock	il vient de recevoir un choc électrique	eel vee-iN de re-ce-vwahr (ai)N shok ay-laik-treek

CALLING FOR HELP

DEMANDER DE L'AIDE

d'maN-day d'layd

Please call for . . .	Veuillez appeler	v(ai)-yay ahp-lay
a doctor	un docteur	(ai)N dok-t(ai)r
an ambulance	une ambulance	(ee)n aN-b(ee)-laNs
a rescue party	des secours	day s'koor
the fire brigade	les pompiers	lay poN-pyay
the coastguards	les garde-côtes	lay gahrd coht
the air-sea rescue	les secours aéronavale	lay s'koor ah-ay-roh-nah-vahl

In most large towns in France, POLICE-SECOURS can be obtained by dialling 17, and the fire brigade (LES POMPIERS) by dialling 18. However, in small rural areas, it is advisable to check these numbers with the local exchange, and get them to put you through. If you propose to live in one place for any length of time, it would be highly advisable to enquire immediately on arrival what are the relevant numbers for Police and Fire Services.

THE SUNSHINE PHRASE BOOKS

Uniform with this book

Sunshine German Phrase Book
Sunshine French Phrase Book
Sunshine Italian Phrase Book
Sunshine Spanish Phrase Book

Some paperfronts are listed on the following pages. A full list of the titles currently available can be had by sending a stamped addressed envelope to:

Elliot Right Way Books, Lower Kingswood, Tadworth, Surrey, U.K.